DR. OLIVIA CAR

ZERO POINT WEIGHT LOSS

Cookbook

The Ultimate Guide to Slimming Easily & Enjoyable. Cook Delicious, Healthy Meal Without Stress, Guilt-Free & Counting Calories Simple, Quick and Easy Cooking Recipes No Point. 30-Day Meal Plan & Nutrition Guide

Copyright Page

Disclaimer

Table *of* Content

CHAPTER 1: INTRODUCTION
1.1 What Are Zero Point Foods?

Imagine standing in your kitchen, surrounded by vibrant colors and tantalizing aromas. The sun streams through the window, casting a warm glow on a colorful array of fresh vegetables and fruits. You reach for a crisp bell pepper, its crunch promising a burst of flavor, and you realize you can enjoy it without a second thought about calories or points. Welcome to the world of Zero Point Foods—a culinary paradise where health meets freedom.

Zero Point Foods are the stars of the Weight Watchers program, revolutionizing the way we think about dieting. These foods, which include a variety of fruits, vegetables, lean proteins, and legumes, hold the incredible power of Zero Points. This means you can savor them freely, liberating you from the constraints of traditional dieting. Picture indulging in a hearty bowl of vegetable soup, packed with leafy greens and vibrant tomatoes, all while knowing that you're nourishing your body without guilt. It's not just a meal; it's a celebration of flavor and wellness.

At the heart of this concept is a simple yet profound truth: eating healthy doesn't have to be a chore. With Zero Point Foods, you can create delicious, satisfying meals that fuel your body and satisfy your cravings. The beauty lies in their nutrient density—these foods are not only low in calories but also packed with essential vitamins, minerals, and fiber. They help you feel full and energized, making it easier to resist those tempting sugary snacks that often derail our efforts.

Imagine whipping up a refreshing salad bursting with colors—crunchy cucumbers, juicy strawberries, and a sprinkle of vibrant herbs. You can drizzle it with a homemade dressing made from zero-point ingredients, creating a dish that looks as good as it tastes. Each bite is a reminder that healthy eating can be an adventure, not a punishment.

Moreover, the inclusion of Zero Point Foods promotes a positive relationship with food. You're encouraged to embrace your hunger cues, to listen to your body, and to enjoy meals without the weight of guilt. This shift in mindset transforms the act of eating from a stressful obligation into a joyful experience. The more you indulge in these foods, the more you realize that they not only satisfy your appetite but also nurture your body and spirit.

In a world where diets are often associated with deprivation and sacrifice, Zero Point Foods stand out as a refreshing alternative. They invite you to explore a palette of flavors and textures, empowering you to create meals that reflect your personal taste and lifestyle. So, step into your kitchen with confidence, knowing that every choice you make is a step toward a healthier, happier you.

The journey toward health and wellness is not just about numbers; it's about finding joy in the process. With Zero Point Foods, you have the freedom to enjoy your meals fully, indulge in flavors you love, and ultimately cultivate a lifestyle that feels rewarding. Embrace this delicious journey, and let Zero Point Foods guide you to a life where health and happiness coexist harmoniously.

In our Zero Point Weight Loss Cookbook, you'll find an array of recipes that celebrate these nourishing ingredients, helping you make the most of the Zero Point system while enjoying every step of your culinary adventure.

1.2. History and Development of the Zero Point Diet

In this book, «Zero Point Weight Loss Cookbook» we aim to introduce readers to the renowned weight loss system developed by Weight Watchers, now known as WW. Founded by Jean Nidetch in the early 1960s, this program has transformed the way individuals approach healthy living and weight management.

The Birth of Weight Watchers
The journey began in 1963 when Jean Nidetch, a New York housewife, started hosting informal gatherings in her home. Frustrated with traditional dieting methods that often left her feeling deprived and isolated, Nidetch created a supportive environment where friends and neighbors could share their weight loss experiences. This concept of community support became a cornerstone of the program and quickly resonated with many others seeking similar solutions.

Nidetch's initiative led to the establishment of the first official Weight Watchers meeting in Queens, New York. Understanding that accountability and shared experiences are vital for success, she laid the groundwork for a structured program centered on healthy eating and lifestyle choices.

Introduction of the Zero Points Concept
As the program evolved, so did its methodologies. One of the pivotal innovations was the introduction of the Zero Points foods list, designed to encourage members to consume nutrient-dense options without the pressure of counting points. This concept is rooted in the idea that certain foods—primarily fruits, vegetables, and lean proteins—are not only low in calories but also high in vitamins and minerals.

By promoting a variety of Zero Points foods, WW aimed to help members cultivate a healthier relationship with food. The initiative was built on the understanding that these foods can satisfy hunger, curb cravings, and support overall weight loss efforts without the guilt that often accompanies traditional dieting.

The Zero Points concept has remained integral to WW's philosophy, adapting to meet the changing needs of its members. It reinforces the message that healthy eating can be both enjoyable and accessible, allowing individuals to fill their plates with wholesome options.

In this cookbook, we do not claim to have invented the Zero Points system or the methodologies developed by Weight Watchers. Instead, our goal is to familiarize you with these concepts and provide you with practical recipes and tips to integrate Zero Points foods into your meals.

CHAPTER 2
FEATURES OF THE ZERO-POINT FOOD SYSTEM

2.1. Health Advantages of Zero-Point Foods

Including Zero-Point foods in your diet offers a wealth of health benefits that extend far beyond weight loss. Chosen for their low-calorie count and nutrient-rich profiles, these foods are designed to support overall health and vitality. Adding a variety of Zero-Point foods to your meals helps fuel your body for optimal functioning and assists in weight management naturally and sustainably.

One major advantage of these foods is their high fiber content, with both soluble and insoluble fiber types offering unique benefits. Soluble fiber, abundant in fruits, vegetables, and legumes, dissolves in water to form a gel-like substance in the gut. This process slows digestion and helps regulate blood sugar levels by stabilizing the release of sugars, making it easier to manage hunger and sustain energy throughout the day. Insoluble fiber, also found in these foods, aids in promoting regularity and preventing constipation, which supports a balanced gut microbiome and digestive health.

Zero-Point foods are packed with essential vitamins and minerals that contribute to daily health and energy levels. Fruits like berries, oranges, and apples deliver vitamin C, which bolsters immune function and aids in collagen production for healthy skin. Leafy greens such as spinach and kale provide vitamins A and K, essential for vision and bone health, respectively. Additionally, minerals like potassium—found in foods like bananas and tomatoes—play crucial roles in maintaining muscle and nerve function, balancing body fluids, and supporting cardiovascular health by regulating blood pressure.

Lean proteins, including skinless chicken, turkey, fish, and legumes, provide the essential amino acids needed for muscle repair and growth. By supporting muscle maintenance, these proteins also promote metabolic health, as muscle tissue burns more calories than fat. Protein's role in satiety is equally important; it helps reduce cravings and keeps you feeling fuller for longer, especially when paired with fiber-rich foods, making it easier to control portion sizes and stick to dietary goals.

Non-fat dairy products like yogurt and quark offer the benefits of calcium and probiotics. Calcium is vital for maintaining strong bones and teeth, while probiotics support gut health by promoting a balanced microbiome. These dairy products also bring creaminess to dishes without adding excess calories, making them versatile additions to a satisfying and nutritious meal plan.

Lastly, Zero-Point foods are rich in antioxidants, including vitamin C, vitamin E, and beta-carotene, found in colorful fruits and leafy greens. These antioxidants combat free radicals that cause cellular damage, supporting healthier aging and reducing the risk of chronic diseases like heart disease and cancer. This defense against oxidative stress, along with the combined benefits of fiber, lean proteins, and essential vitamins, makes Zero-Point foods a powerful foundation for both health and weight management.

2.2. Fundamental Principles of zero point food & Benefits

The Zero Point Diet, as part of the Weight Watchers program, is built on a foundation that promotes healthy eating, sustainable weight management, and a positive relationship with food. Zero Point Foods encourage a balanced, flexible, and fulfilling approach to nutrition. Here are the essential principles and benefits that define this diet:

1. Zero Point Foods as a Foundation

Zero Point Foods are the core of this diet, offering a variety of nutrient-dense, low-calorie foods that can be enjoyed freely, without the need to count calories or track every bite.

Key Categories of Zero Point Foods

Fruits: Fresh, naturally sweet, and fiber-rich, fruits like apples, bananas, berries, and tropical options (e.g., mangoes and pineapples) satisfy cravings without guilt. Their natural sugars provide quick energy, while their fiber content supports digestion and sustained fullness.

Non-Starchy Vegetables: These nutrient powerhouses, including leafy greens, cruciferous veggies (like broccoli and cauliflower), and colorful roots (like carrots and radishes), offer vitamins and antioxidants essential for immunity and digestive health. With their low-calorie density, they add volume to meals, keeping you full longer.

Beans and Legumes: Beans, lentils, and peas are rich in protein and soluble fiber, promoting satiety and stable blood sugar levels. From versatile black beans to protein-packed chickpeas, these options are perfect for soups, salads, and hearty main dishes.

Lean Proteins: Skinless chicken and turkey breast, eggs, and seafood provide essential amino acids for muscle repair and growth. Their high-protein content keeps you energized and supports metabolism, while their low-fat profile ensures you stay on track with your dietary goals.

Nonfat Dairy and Plant-Based Yogurt: Options like nonfat Greek yogurt, plain soy yogurt, and cottage cheese (0% fat) offer protein, probiotics, and calcium, supporting bone health and digestion. These creamy additions are ideal for breakfast bowls, smoothies, or healthy dips.

By focusing on these Zero Point Foods, the diet encourages a simple and nutritious way of eating, promoting health and wellness without the burden of calorie counting.

In Chapter 6, Bonus Materials, you will find a comprehensive and detailed list of Zero-Point foods (ready to print).

2. Enhanced Fullness and Appetite Control

Zero Point Foods are generally high in fiber, protein, and water content, keeping you satisfied for longer periods. This natural fullness reduces cravings and helps prevent overeating, making it easier to stay on track with your goals.

3. Mindful Eating Practices

The Zero Point Diet promotes mindfulness in eating habits by encouraging individuals to:
Listen to Hunger Cues: Recognize true hunger versus emotional eating.
Savor Each Bite: Take time to enjoy the taste and texture of food, increasing satisfaction and reducing the tendency to overeat.
Avoid Distractions: Focus on meals without screens or multitasking, enhancing the connection with food and satisfaction.

Mindful eating fosters a healthier relationship with food, reducing guilt and promoting more balanced eating habits.

4. Flexibility and Variety in Food Choices

With a diverse array of Zero Point Foods, the diet offers flexibility that suits a variety of dietary preferences and needs. This versatility enables:

Exploration of New Flavors: Experimenting with different cuisines, cooking methods, and recipes prevents meal fatigue.
Creative Substitutions: Replace high-calorie ingredients with Zero Point alternatives, allowing for enjoyable meals without compromising flavor.

Flexibility supports individuals in various situations, like social gatherings or dining out, helping maintain dietary goals while enjoying the journey.

5. Ease of Meal Planning and Preparation

Zero Point Foods simplify meal planning by eliminating the need for constant tracking. This ease allows individuals to focus on enjoying the cooking process and preparing nutritious, home-cooked meals, which are often healthier than takeout options.

6. Reduces Diet-Related Stress

The Zero Point Diet offers a relief from the pressures of constant calorie counting and tracking. By allowing individuals to eat freely from a selection of satisfying, low-calorie foods, it reduces the stress and anxiety often associated with restrictive diets. This freedom encourages:

A Relaxed Approach to Eating: With fewer rules and restrictions, individuals can focus on enjoying their meals without guilt or worry.

Positive Food Relationship: The reduced stress fosters a balanced and intuitive connection with food, making it easier to sustain a healthy lifestyle over time.

This approach contributes to an overall sense of well-being and makes it easier to adhere to the diet long-term.

7. Support for Sustainable Weight Management

The Zero Point Diet is structured to facilitate lasting weight management rather than quick fixes. By prioritizing foods that are naturally low in calories, it helps create a caloric balance without feeling restricted. This approach supports:

Balanced Nutrition: Creating meals that meet nutritional needs without the pressure of counting calories.
Healthy Long-Term Habits: Developing habits that lead to sustainable weight loss and prevent yo-yo dieting.

8. Community and Support Network

The Weight Watchers community is a valuable component of the Zero Point Diet. Through meetings, online forums, and social media groups, individuals benefit from:

Shared Experiences: Connecting with others on a similar journey fosters motivation, accountability, and encouragement.
Learning and Growth: Exchanging recipes, tips, and stories provides a sense of camaraderie and helps members stay engaged.

This support network can significantly enhance the diet experience, creating lasting connections and reinforcing commitment.

9. Holistic Focus on Health and Wellness

While weight loss is a goal, the Zero Point Diet also emphasizes overall health, both physical and emotional:

Holistic Approach: Encourages physical health along with mental well-being, including regular activity, self-care, and stress management.
Positive Mindset: Fostering a positive relationship with food and body image, the diet helps focus on health, not just numbers on a scale.

This approach encourages long-term success by promoting a balanced, joyful relationship with food.

2.3. Zero Point Meal Planning

Effective meal planning is a cornerstone of successful weight management and a healthy lifestyle, especially when focusing on Zero Point foods. By organizing your meals around these nutrient-dense options, you can create satisfying, balanced dishes that align with your goals while making the process enjoyable and stress-free. Here's how to approach meal planning with Zero Point foods in mind.

Creating Balanced Meals

To build balanced meals using Zero Point foods, consider the following components:

1. Base: Start with a foundation of Zero Point vegetables. Fill your plate with colorful, nutrient-rich options such as leafy greens, bell peppers, and broccoli. These vegetables provide essential vitamins and minerals while keeping calorie counts low.

2. Protein: Next, incorporate a lean protein source from the Zero Point category. Options like grilled chicken, fish, or legumes can add satisfying protein to your meal. Aim for about a quarter of your plate to be filled with protein to support muscle maintenance and keep you feeling full.

3. Healthy Fats: While not all fats are Zero Point, you can include small portions of healthy fats, such as avocado, olive oil, or nuts, to enhance flavor and satisfaction. These can be measured to fit within your Points allowance, ensuring that you enjoy the health benefits without overindulging.

Planning for the Week

1. Set Aside Time: Dedicate a specific time each week to plan your meals. This could be a Sunday afternoon or any day that suits your schedule. Use this time to reflect on your week ahead, consider your schedule, and decide when you will need quick meals versus more elaborate cooking sessions.

2. Choose Your Recipes: Select a variety of recipes that utilize Zero Point foods, ensuring a mix of flavors and textures. Aim for a balance between different food categories—fruits, vegetables, proteins, and grains. This variety will keep your meals interesting and satisfying.

3. Make a Shopping List: After selecting your recipes, create a detailed shopping list. Include all the ingredients you'll need for the week, focusing on fresh produce, lean proteins, and pantry staples. Having a well-organized list can streamline your grocery shopping and reduce impulse buys.

4. Batch Cooking: Consider batch cooking some of your meals or components ahead of time. For example, you can cook a large batch of quinoa or roast a variety of vegetables to use throughout the week. This preparation not only saves time but also makes it easier to assemble meals quickly.

5. Flexible Approach: While having a meal plan is essential, it's equally important to remain flexible. Life can be unpredictable, so be prepared to adapt your plans as needed. If a recipe doesn't fit your schedule one night, swap it with a quicker option that utilizes similar ingredients.

Using Leftovers Wisely

One of the benefits of meal planning is the ability to repurpose leftovers creatively:

Transformative Recipes: Use leftover grilled chicken in a salad or wrap, or incorporate extra roasted vegetables into a frittata. This not only minimizes food waste but also saves time on cooking.
Freezing for Later: If you prepare more than you can consume within a week, consider freezing portions for future meals. This is particularly useful for soups and stews, which often taste even better after sitting for a day or two.

Snacks and In-Between Meals
Don't forget to plan for snacks and small meals throughout the day. ZeroPoint foods make excellent snack options that can help you stay satisfied between meals. Here are a few ideas:

Fruit and Nut Butter: Pair apple slices with a small amount of almond or peanut butter.
Vegetable Sticks and Hummus: Enjoy carrot and cucumber sticks with a flavorful hummus dip.
Greek Yogurt with Berries: Top plain Greek yogurt with fresh berries for a quick and nutritious snack.

Incorporating Zero Point foods into your meal planning can significantly enhance your weight management efforts and promote a healthy lifestyle. By focusing on balanced meals, preparing in advance, and using leftovers creatively, you can make the process enjoyable and sustainable. With a well-structured meal plan, you'll find it easier to stay on track while enjoying a variety of delicious, nutrient-dense foods that support your health and wellness goals. Embrace the journey of meal planning, and let it empower you to cultivate a positive relationship with food.

In Chapter 5, Bonus Materials, you will find a ready-to-use 30-day meal plan.
In Chapter 6 Bonus Materials you will find a 30-day meal plan (ready to print).

2.4. What Helps Accelerate Weight Loss?

Embarking on a weight loss journey can be challenging, but incorporating a variety of methods for movement, proper hydration, and practical strategies can significantly enhance your progress. In this section, we'll explore different forms of physical activity, the importance of staying hydrated, and additional strategies to help you reach your weight loss goals.

1. Varied Forms of Movement

Incorporating different forms of movement into your daily routine can help accelerate weight loss and improve overall health. Here are some effective methods:

Fitness Walking: Walking is one of the simplest and most effective exercises. Aim for brisk walks that elevate your heart rate. Start with 30 minutes a day, gradually increasing your duration and intensity.

Running or Jogging: If you're looking for a more intense workout, consider adding running or jogging to your routine. This high-impact exercise burns more calories in a shorter period and can be easily integrated into your day.

Group Sports: Participating in group sports like soccer, basketball, or volleyball not only provides a great workout but also makes exercising fun and social. Engaging in team activities can keep you motivated and accountable.

Dance Classes: Whether it's Zumba, hip-hop, or salsa, dancing is an enjoyable way to burn calories while having fun. Plus, it can improve coordination and flexibility.

Strength Training: Incorporating weight lifting or bodyweight exercises can help build muscle, which in turn increases your resting metabolic rate. Consider doing push-ups, squats, or using resistance bands at home or the gym.

Playful Activities: Don't underestimate the value of playful movement! Activities like jumping rope, playing tag with kids, or even dancing around your living room can significantly contribute to your daily physical activity.

Gentle Movements: If you prefer lower-impact activities, consider yoga or Pilates. These exercises not only enhance flexibility and core strength but also promote mindfulness and stress relief.

The Power of Walking: A Simple Path to Wellness

Walking is a versatile, highly effective, and often underrated exercise that promotes both overall wellness and weight loss. Let's explore the transformative benefits of aiming for 10,000 steps a day:

Caloric Burn: Walking 10,000 steps can burn between 300 and 500 calories, which helps you achieve a calorie deficit for weight loss.

Cardiovascular Health: Regular walking strengthens the heart, improves circulation, and lowers the risk of heart disease.

Mental Clarity and Mood: Walking reduces stress, boosts mood, and provides a mental reset. The rhythm of walking can stimulate creativity and problem-solving.

Muscle and Bone Strength: Walking engages various muscle groups and strengthens bones, reducing the risk of osteoporosis.

Energy Boost: Walking enhances blood flow and oxygen delivery to muscles, increasing overall energy.

Social Interaction: Walking with friends or a group can make the activity more enjoyable and provide motivation.

Walking as Meditation
Walking can serve as a moving meditation. This involves being mindful of each step, connecting with your surroundings, and practicing rhythmic breathing. It helps promote relaxation, mental clarity, and space for self-reflection, transforming each walk into a calming, health-promoting activity.

Walking is a simple yet effective way to enhance your health. Striving for 10,000 steps a day can boost your physical fitness and promote mental well-being. Embrace walking as part of your daily routine and enjoy the journey toward a healthier, happier you!

In Chapter 6, Bonus Materials, you will find a 10,000 Steps-a-Day Tracker.

2. Hydration

Staying hydrated is essential for effective weight loss and overall health. Here's how proper hydration can support your efforts:

Metabolism Boost: Drinking enough water can temporarily increase your metabolism. Studies show that consuming about 500 ml of water can elevate your metabolic rate by 30% for approximately 30-40 minutes.

Hunger Control: Sometimes, our bodies mistake thirst for hunger. Drinking water before meals can help control appetite and make it easier to stick to portion sizes.

Improved Exercise Performance: Proper hydration can enhance your physical performance. When well-hydrated, you'll have more e nergy and stamina for activities, making workouts more effective.

Daily Hydration Goal: Aim for at least 8 glasses (1,5 - 2 liters) of water per day. Use reminders or apps to help you stay on track.

In Chapter 6, Bonus Materials, you will find a Daily Water Intake Tracker.

By incorporating a variety of movement methods, maintaining proper hydration, and implementing practical strategies, you can accelerate your weight loss efforts and create a healthier lifestyle. These simple adjustments complement the Zero Point system and help you stay focused on your goals. Embrace these strategies, and take confident steps toward achieving a healthier, happier you. Remember, every bit of movement contributes to your overall success on this rewarding path to wellness.

2.5 Embracing the Zero Point Lifestyle

The Zero Point system goes beyond being a simple diet—it's a comprehensive lifestyle approach designed to empower you to take charge of your health and well-being. By embracing its principles, you move past temporary fixes and restrictive eating, stepping into a world where nourishing your body becomes both joyful and deeply satisfying.

The Zero Point lifestyle invites you to cultivate a positive relationship with food, allowing you to enjoy a wide variety of delicious meals without the burden of guilt or calorie counting. This system equips you with the knowledge and tools to make informed choices, helping you navigate your eating habits with confidence.

Once you grasp the core concepts of Zero Point foods and their benefits, you'll find that maintaining a healthy lifestyle becomes second nature. You'll learn to listen to your body's hunger cues, make mindful food choices, and appreciate the flavors and textures of your meals. This newfound understanding enables you to control your eating patterns and achieve your weight loss goals sustainably.

Remember, the journey to wellness is about progress, not perfection. Embrace the Zero Point lifestyle as a commitment to yourself, focusing on long-term health rather than short-term results. By integrating these principles into your daily routine, you can create a balanced, enjoyable way of living that celebrates food and nourishes your body.

CHAPTER 3
ZERO POINT KITCHEN: TOOLS, TECHNIQUES AND ORGANIZATION

Chapter 3.1: Cooking Techniques and Tips

Mastering the right cooking techniques is essential when preparing Zero Point foods. These methods not only preserve the nutrients in your meals but also bring out the natural flavors of the ingredients without adding unnecessary calories. In this section, we will explore healthy cooking methods, essential kitchen tools, and flavor enhancement tips that will elevate your experience with Zero Point foods. Let's dive into each technique, making sure you maximize the nutritional value while keeping your meals delicious and satisfying.

Healthy Cooking Methods

1. Steaming
Steaming is one of the healthiest cooking methods as it preserves the nutrients in vegetables, keeping them tender and vibrant. When you steam, the water never touches the food, ensuring that vitamins and minerals remain intact. This method is particularly effective for cooking Zero Point vegetables such as broccoli, carrots, and asparagus, ensuring that they maintain their crispness and flavor.

Tip: Use a steamer basket over boiling water, or if you don't have a dedicated steamer, a colander or sieve over a pot works perfectly. For added flavor, season the veggies with a squeeze of lemon or a sprinkle of fresh herbs.

2. Roasting
Roasting vegetables brings out their natural sweetness and creates a caramelized texture that enhances their flavor. It's an excellent way to prepare Zero Point vegetables like bell peppers, zucchini, and sweet potatoes. Roasting requires minimal oil, keeping the calorie count low, while intensifying the flavors of the ingredients.

Tip: Toss your vegetables with a small amount of olive oil (if using), or skip the oil altogether and use a light spray of cooking spray. Add your favorite spices like paprika or garlic powder before roasting to create a flavorful dish without extra calories. Bake at 375°F for about 20-25 minute or until golden brown.

3. Grilling
Grilling infuses a smoky flavor into proteins and vegetables. This method works especially well for lean proteins like chicken breast, shrimp, and vegetables. Grilled vegetables, like zucchini, mushrooms, and bell peppers, offer a delightful texture and flavor. Grilled lean proteins like skinless chicken or fish are flavorful, filling, and perfect for a Zero Point meal.

Tip: Marinate your proteins in herbs and spices to infuse them with flavor before grilling. Consider using a grill pan or an outdoor grill for that smoky, charred flavor that adds depth to your dishes. Remember to use minimal oil while grilling to keep your meals light and healthy.

4. Sautéing

Sautéing is a quick and simple cooking method that involves cooking food in a small amount of oil or cooking spray over medium-high heat. This technique is perfect for Zero Point vegetables like spinach, mushrooms, and onions. Sautéing locks in the natural flavors of these ingredients and helps them retain their texture.

Tip: Use non-stick pans to minimize the amount of oil needed. If you prefer not to use oil, opt for vegetable or chicken broth to sauté your veggies. Add fresh garlic, herbs, or a dash of soy sauce for a flavor boost.

5. Baking

Baking is perfect for creating hearty dishes like casseroles or baked vegetables. You can make a Zero Point vegetable lasagna using whole-grain noodles, zucchini, and mushrooms, or bake a flavorful frittata with lean proteins and Zero Point vegetables. This method allows you to create filling meals that are satisfying yet low in calories.

Tip: For baked dishes, consider using parchment paper to line your baking dish to prevent sticking and avoid using excess oil or butter. You can also sprinkle a small amount of non-fat cheese to enhance the flavor without adding extra calories.

6. Boiling

Boiling is one of the most straightforward methods, especially for grains like brown rice or quinoa, and for boiling vegetables like carrots or peas. When done correctly, boiling helps preserve the flavor and nutrients of the ingredients. It's perfect for creating the base of a hearty soup or a nutritious grain bowl.

Tip: Make sure not to overcook your grains or vegetables to avoid losing vital nutrients. After boiling, consider using some of the cooking liquid in soups or sauces to maximize the flavor. For grains, follow package instructions for perfect texture and consistency.

Essential Kitchen Tools

Having the right kitchen tools can make meal preparation quicker, easier, and more enjoyable, especially when working with Zero Point ingredients. Below is a list of essential tools that will help you make the most of your Zero Point meals:

Steamer Basket

A steamer basket is ideal for steaming vegetables while preserving their nutrients. A collapsible basket can fit into various pot sizes, making it versatile for different meals. If you want to create fresh, crisp vegetables or fish, this is a must-have tool in your kitchen.

Non-Stick Cookware

Investing in good-quality non-stick cookware is a game-changer when cooking Zero Point foods. It allows you to cook with minimal oil, keeping meals lighter and healthier without compromising on flavor. Non-stick pans are especially useful for sautéing vegetables or making quick stir-fries.

Blender or Food Processor

A blender or food processor is essential for making smoothies, soups, sauces, or even doughs. It will save you time when you need to puree vegetables or mix ingredients for recipes like Zero Point smoothies or hummus. These gadgets also make it easier to prep ingredients like herbs, spices, and even fruits for fresh salads.

Spiralizer

A spiralizer is a fun tool for turning vegetables like zucchini, carrots, or sweet potatoes into low-calorie "noodles." This is perfect for replacing traditional pasta with a Zero Point alternative. You can also use the spiralized veggies in salads or as a base for stir-fries.

Measuring Cups and Spoons

Accurate measurements are important for portion control, especially when tracking your Zero Point foods. Using measuring cups and spoons helps ensure that your meals are well-balanced and help you avoid overeating. This is also important when preparing recipes that need precise ingredients to maintain the integrity of the Zero Point system.

Cutting Board and Sharp Knives

A sturdy cutting board and sharp knives are essential for efficient food preparation. With these tools, you'll be able to chop, slice, and dice your ingredients with ease. A good knife set can make meal prep more efficient and safe.

Oven Mitts and Baking Sheets

For roasting and baking, investing in oven mitts and baking sheets ensures safety and proper cooking. Good-quality baking sheets prevent sticking and allow for even cooking of Zero Point vegetables and proteins.

Mixing Bowls: A set of mixing bowls in various sizes is useful for combining ingredients, marinating proteins, and preparing salads.

Flavor Enhancement Tips

Flavoring your meals without adding extra calories is crucial in making Zero Point foods satisfying. Here are some flavor-enhancing techniques and ingredients to try:

Herbs and Spices

Fresh and dried herbs are your best friends when cooking Zero Point meals. They are an easy way to add flavor without calories. Consider using basil, cilantro, parsley, or dill to brighten up your dishes. Spices like cumin, paprika, turmeric, and cayenne pepper can add depth and warmth to your meals. The key is experimenting with combinations to find flavors you love.

Citrus Zest and Juice

Citrus zest and juice are perfect for adding a burst of freshness to your meals. A squeeze of lemon or lime juice can elevate the flavor of your dishes, while the zest adds an aromatic touch. Try using citrus in dressings, marinades, or as a finishing touch on your meals for an extra layer of flavor.

Low-Calorie Sauces and Dressings

Create your own sauces using Zero Point ingredients like non-fat Greek yogurt, lemon juice, and herbs. This way, you can control the ingredients and keep your meals light. For example, make a creamy dressing using Greek yogurt and fresh herbs like parsley and dill for a guilt-free, flavorful addition to your salads.

Umami Boosters

Umami is the savory taste that adds depth to your meals. Nutritional yeast, miso paste, and low-sodium soy sauce are great options for boosting umami flavor without adding significant calories. These ingredients can elevate the savory profile of soups, stews, and other dishes.

Meal Assembly Tips

Layering Flavors

When assembling a dish, think about how to layer flavors for maximum impact. Start with a base of Zero Point vegetables or grains, add roasted or steamed vegetables for texture, and top with a lean protein. Finish off with a drizzle of a low-calorie sauce or a sprinkle of fresh herbs for added flavor.

Color and Texture

Aim for a variety of colors and textures on your plate. A visually appealing meal enhances the overall experience and can make the meal feel more satisfying. Combine crunchy vegetables like carrots or bell peppers with creamy dressings or tender proteins like chicken or fish for a delightful contrast.

Portion Control

While Zero Point foods allow for generous portions, it's still important to be mindful of your serving sizes. Use smaller plates or bowls to help control portions and prevent overeating, even with healthy foods. This ensures that you can enjoy your meals without overindulging.

Presentation Matters

Don't forget about the importance of presentation. A beautifully arranged plate can make even the simplest dish feel more special. Garnish your dishes with fresh herbs, a sprinkle of seeds, or a drizzle of sauce for an extra touch of flair.

By mastering these cooking techniques, using the right kitchen tools, and enhancing your meals with delicious seasonings, you'll be well on your way to making Zero Point foods a regular part of your healthy lifestyle. With these tips, preparing nutritious meals becomes not only easy but enjoyable. Each meal is an opportunity to create something vibrant, delicious, and good for your body.

3.2. Organizing Your Kitchen for Efficient Cooking on a Zero Point Diet

Creating a functional and organized kitchen is a cornerstone of success when adopting a Zero Point diet. A well-arranged cooking space not only simplifies meal prep but also makes the entire process more enjoyable and less stressful. By setting up your kitchen efficiently, you'll spend less time looking for tools and ingredients and more time creating delicious, nutritious meals. Let's explore how you can organize your kitchen for maximum efficiency and enjoyability.

1. Declutter Your Space

Before you begin cooking, take some time to declutter your kitchen. A clutter-free environment allows you to focus on the task at hand and speeds up meal prep. Here's how to start:

Frequency of Use: Organize your kitchen based on how often you use your items. Keep everyday tools like knives, cutting boards, measuring spoons, and mixing bowls within easy reach. Items used less frequently, such as specialty appliances or bakeware, should be stored in higher cabinets or deeper drawers.

Storage Solutions: Use drawer dividers, shelf organizers, and baskets to sort your utensils, pots, and pans. A magnetic strip for knives or metal utensils can free up valuable drawer space while keeping them easily accessible. Consider using clear containers for frequently used pantry staples to ensure you're always prepared to create meals without delay.

Purge Expired Ingredients: Regularly go through your pantry, fridge, and freezer to check for expired or unwanted items. Discarding old ingredients makes space for fresh ones and prevents using food that's no longer safe. This practice also encourages you to use ingredients before they go bad, promoting a zero-waste environment.

2. Designate Zones for Cooking Tasks

Designating specific zones within your kitchen ensures that everything you need is within arm's reach, making cooking more efficient and enjoyable.

Preparation Zone: Set up a dedicated area for chopping, slicing, and mixing. Keep your cutting boards, knives, vegetable peeler, and measuring cups here. If possible, also have a trash bin or compost bin nearby to easily dispose of waste as you go.

Cooking Zone: Store your pots, pans, utensils, and spatulas near the stove or oven. When everything is within reach, you won't waste time rummaging through drawers. If you often use specific pans or tools, place them in the most accessible drawers or cabinets.

Serving Zone: Organize your serving dishes, bowls, and utensils in a designated spot, ensuring that they're easily accessible when it's time to plate your meals. This reduces unnecessary steps when you're ready to serve and ensures your meal is plated quickly and elegantly.

3. Use Clear Containers for Ingredients

Clear, labeled containers are key to maintaining an organized and efficient kitchen. They help you quickly identify what's available in your pantry or fridge and encourage you to use what you have before it expires.

Mason Jars & Airtight Containers: These are perfect for storing dry goods like grains, beans, and spices. The airtight seals help keep food fresh for longer periods, and clear jars allow you to quickly see the contents, so you don't forget what you have on hand.

Labeling: Make sure to label all containers, especially if they are stored in bulk. Use a label maker or chalkboard labels to mark what's inside and when it was purchased. This helps with both organization and ensuring you use your ingredients before they expire.

4. Plan Your Meals with Accessibility in Mind

Efficient meal planning is essential for Zero Point success. Plan ahead so that your kitchen is ready for quick cooking and minimal stress. Consider the following tips:

Prep Ahead: Set aside a couple of hours each week to prep your ingredients. Wash, chop, and store vegetables and proteins in ready-to-use portions. This will save time during the week and help you avoid the temptation to order takeout.

Batch Cooking: Prepare larger quantities of Zero Point meals that can be easily reheated throughout the week. For example, cook a large pot of soup or stew, or bake a casserole that can be stored in individual portions. Use clear, labeled containers to store these meals in the fridge or freezer for easy access.

One-Pot Meals: Consider investing in a slow cooker or Instant Pot for quick and easy one-pot meals. These devices allow you to prepare large quantities of Zero Point meals with minimal cleanup and hands-off cooking. Throw in your ingredients in the morning, and by dinner time, you'll have a nutritious, flavorful meal ready to serve.

5. Incorporate Smart Kitchen Gadgets

Utilizing the right kitchen gadgets can save you time and effort, making meal prep easier and more enjoyable. Here are some tools that will enhance your Zero Point cooking experience:

Food Processor: Perfect for quickly chopping vegetables, making sauces, or blending soups. A food processor can handle time-consuming tasks like mincing garlic or chopping herbs, making meal prep much faster.

Instant Thermometer: An instant read thermometer ensures that your meals are cooked to perfection. It helps prevent overcooking or undercooking, especially with proteins, reducing food waste and making your meals more flavorful.

Digital Kitchen Scale: A digital scale helps with precise portion control, which is essential for Zero Point tracking. It ensures you are measuring your ingredients accurately, especially when working with grains, proteins, and other components that need careful portioning.

6. Create a Visual Meal Planner

A visual meal planner is a great way to keep your meals organized and motivate you to stay on track with your Zero Point goals.

Inspiration Board: Use a bulletin board or dry erase board to post your planned meals for the week. Include recipes, shopping lists, and inspiration for new dishes. This visual reminder keeps you excited and organized as you tackle your meal prep.

Motivational Quotes and Photos: Add some motivational quotes or images of healthy meals to keep your spirits high and encourage you throughout the week. Visual reminders can make cooking feel less like a chore and more like an exciting part of your day.

7. Keep It Fun and Engaging

Creating an enjoyable cooking experience is key to sticking with your Zero Point journey. Here's how to keep the process fun:

Play Music or Podcasts: Set the mood in your kitchen by playing your favorite tunes or an interesting podcast. This turns meal prep into a relaxing, enjoyable activity and helps make the time go by quickly.

Involve Family or Friends: Get others involved in the cooking process. Assign tasks like washing vegetables, stirring, or setting the table to make cooking a team effort. This not only saves you time but also makes it a more engaging and collaborative experience.

A well-organized kitchen is one of the best tools you can have when following a Zero Point diet. By decluttering your space, creating designated cooking zones, and utilizing the right kitchen tools, you'll be able to prepare meals more efficiently and enjoy the cooking process.

3.3. Zero Point Food Storage and Purchasing

Proper purchasing and storage techniques are crucial for maintaining the quality, flavor, and nutritional value of Zero Point foods. By following these strategies, you can maximize the freshness of your ingredients, minimize waste, and ensure that you're always ready to prepare healthy, Zero Point meals.

Purchasing Strategies

1. Plan Your Grocery Trips

A little planning goes a long way when it comes to shopping for Zero Point foods. Before you head to the store, take some time to plan your meals for the week. Create a detailed shopping list that includes a variety of Zero Point foods—fruits, vegetables, lean proteins, legumes. A list helps you stay focused and prevents impulse buys, making your trip more efficient and cost-effective.

2. Shop Seasonal and Local

Whenever possible, opt for seasonal and locally grown produce. Seasonal fruits and vegetables are usually fresher, more flavorful, and often more affordable than imported options. Visiting farmers' markets or local farm stands can offer you high-quality produce that supports your community and reduces your environmental footprint.

3. Buy in Bulk

Buying items like beans, lentils, and frozen fruits or vegetables in bulk can save you money and reduce packaging waste. Make sure to store these items properly, such as in airtight containers, to keep them fresh for as long as possible. Bulk purchasing is not only cost-effective but also ensures that you have the essentials on hand for a variety of Zero Point meals.

4. Check Expiration Dates

When buying perishable products, always check the expiration or best-before dates. Choose the freshest items available to maximize their nutritional value. This is especially important for dairy, lean proteins, and pre-packaged items. Regularly rotate your pantry and fridge to ensure you're using older items first to avoid waste.

5. Consider Frozen Options

Don't overlook the frozen section. Frozen fruits and vegetables are often flash-frozen at peak ripeness, locking in their nutrients and flavor. Frozen produce is convenient for meal prep, as it can be kept on hand for smoothies, stir-fries, soups, or salads. It's also a great option for Zero Point foods that are out of season, allowing you to enjoy your favorite ingredients year-round.

6. Read Labels Carefully

When purchasing packaged goods, always read the labels. Look for products with no added sugars, preservatives, or unnecessary additives. For canned vegetables and beans, choose low-sodium versions to keep your meals healthy. Understanding labels helps you make better choices and avoid hidden calories or chemicals that can undermine your Zero Point goals.

Storage Techniques

1. Fruits

Room Temperature vs. Refrigeration: Certain fruits, like bananas and avocados, should be stored at room temperature until they ripen, and then moved to the fridge to extend their freshness. Others, like berries and apples, should be stored in the refrigerator to maintain their quality for a longer time.

Separation: Some fruits, such as apples, release ethylene gas, which speeds up the ripening of nearby fruits. Keep ethylene-producing fruits away from those sensitive to it, such as berries, to prevent spoilage.

2. Vegetables

Produce Bags: Store vegetables like lettuce, kale, and spinach in breathable produce bags or containers. This helps maintain moisture and prevents wilting. For leafy greens, wrapping them in a damp paper towel before sealing them in a bag can keep them crisp for a longer time.

Avoid Pre-Washing: Washing vegetables before storing them can add excess moisture, which can promote mold or premature spoilage. Wash them just before use to prolong their freshness.

3. Lean Proteins

Refrigeration: Keep raw lean proteins like chicken, fish, and turkey in the coldest part of your refrigerator. Always store them in airtight containers to minimize exposure to air, which can lead to spoilage.

Freezing for Longevity: Portion out proteins into meal-sized servings before freezing. Wrap them tightly in freezer-safe bags or containers and label with dates to ensure that they stay fresh when defrosted.

4. Legumes and Beans

Dry Beans: Store dry beans in a cool, dry place in airtight containers. If you buy them in bulk, ensure they are properly sealed to prevent moisture and pests.

Canned Beans: Keep canned beans in your pantry and check the expiration dates regularly. Once opened, transfer any leftover beans into an airtight container and refrigerate them.

Additional Tips for Effective Storage

1. Utilize Glass Jars and Containers: Glass jars are perfect for storing grains, beans, spices, and other dry goods. They are airtight, helping to keep food fresh for longer and are also more eco-friendly compared to plastic.

2. Organize Your Pantry: Arrange your pantry in a way that makes sense for the frequency of use. Store items you use daily (like beans and spices) at the front, while less frequently used items can go to the back. Rotate stock to avoid old ingredients being forgotten.

3. Label Everything: Always label your containers with the contents and the date you purchased or stored them. This helps you keep track of what you have and reduces the chances of food waste.

Proper purchasing and storage are essential to making Zero Point foods a sustainable part of your daily routine. By planning your grocery trips, shopping seasonally, buying in bulk, and following smart storage techniques, you can ensure that your ingredients stay fresh and ready to support your healthy eating habits.

CHAPTER 4: RECIPES
4.1 BREAKFASTS

 1. ## Cauliflower Breakfast Porridge with Berries

PREP: 5 MIN   COOK: 10 MIN   SERVINGS: 1

This low-carb breakfast is rich in fiber and vitamins, keeping you full and supporting healthy digestion.

Ingredients:

- 1 cup (100 g) grated cauliflower (fresh or frozen)
- 1/4 cup (60 g) non-fat Greek yogurt
- 1/4 cup (40 g) fresh or frozen berries (blueberries, - strawberries)
- 1/2 tsp cinnamon
- Pinch of vanilla extract (optional)

90 kcal, 6g protein, 1g fat, 10g carbs, 4g fiber

Instructions:

1. Cook the Cauliflower: Bring a small pot of water to a boil. Add the grated cauliflower and cook for 3-4 minutes until tender.

2. Drain and Cool: Drain the cauliflower well and let it cool slightly.

3. Combine Ingredients: In a bowl, mix the cooked cauliflower with Greek yogurt, cinnamon, and vanilla extract until well combined.

4. Garnish and Serve: Top with berries and serve warm.

Tips: Add grated ginger or a sprinkle of lemon zest for an extra burst of flavor. Swap berries for any other ZeroPoint fruits you prefer.

 2. ## Omelette with Turkey, Spinach, and Broccoli

PREP: 5 MIN   COOK: 10 MIN   SERVINGS: 2

This hearty omelette is packed with protein and veggies, perfect for a nutritious start to the day.

Ingredients:

- 4 egg whites (or 2 whole eggs + 2 whites)
- 120 g cooked or roasted turkey, diced
- 1 cup (30 g) fresh spinach
- 1/2 cup (50 g) broccoli

Instructions:

1. Prepare the Ingredients: Blanch the broccoli in boiling water for 2 minutes, then drain.
Rinse and pat dry the spinach.
Dice the turkey into small cubes.

florets, chopped
- 1 clove garlic, minced (optional)
- Pinch of salt
- Pinch of black pepper
- Pinch of paprika (optional)
- 1 tsp water (for fluffiness)
- Cooking spray

2. Whisk the Eggs: In a bowl, whisk the egg whites with a pinch of salt, pepper, paprika, and water until frothy.

3. Cook the Filling: Heat a skillet over medium heat and lightly coat with cooking spray. Sauté the garlic (if using) for 30 seconds.
Add the broccoli and turkey, cooking for 2 minutes while stirring.
Add the spinach and cook for 1 more minute until wilted. Remove the mixture and set aside.

4. Cook the Omelette: In the same skillet, pour the whisked eggs evenly. Cook over medium heat for 2-3 minutes, until the base sets.

5. Add the Filling: Place the turkey, spinach, and broccoli mixture on one side of the omelette. Fold the other side over the filling.

6. Finish Cooking: Cover the skillet with a lid and cook for another 2-3 minutes until the omelette is cooked through.

7. Serve: Slice the omelette in half and serve immediately. Garnish with fresh herbs, if desired.

150 kcal, 20g protein, 4g fat, 4g carbs, 2g fiber

Tips: *Add a squeeze of lemon juice for a fresh touch.*
Spice it up with a drizzle of hot sauce or a sprinkle of chili flakes.

3. Frittata with Broccoli and Tomatoes

PREP: 5 MIN   COOK: 15 MIN   SERVINGS: 2

Broccoli provides fiber and vitamin C, while tomatoes add antioxidants, making this breakfast both nutritious and flavorful.

Ingredients:

- 3 large eggs
- 1/2 cup (50 g) broccoli, chopped
- 1/4 cup (40 g) tomatoes, diced
- 1/4 cup (15 g) green onion, chopped
- Pinch of salt
- Pinch of black pepper
- Cooking spray

Instructions:

1. Preheat the Oven: Set your oven to 180°C (350°F).

2. Cook the Vegetables: Heat a nonstick skillet over medium heat and lightly coat with cooking spray.
Sauté the broccoli and tomatoes for 3-4 minutes until softened.

3. Prepare the Egg Mixture: In a bowl, whisk the eggs with green onion, salt, and black pepper until combined.

4. Combine and Cook: Pour the egg mixture over the vegetables in the skillet, spreading it evenly.

5. Bake the Frittata: Transfer the skillet to the preheated oven. Bake for 10 minutes or until the frittata is set and firm.

6. Serve: Slice into portions and serve hot.

180 kcal, 14g protein,
10g fat, 4g carbs, 2g fiber

Tips: Add a sprinkle of chopped basil or dill for a fresh burst of flavor. Pair with a side of fresh greens for a complete meal.

 ## 4. Fluffy Oven-Baked Omelet

PREP: 5 MIN   COOK: 30 MIN   SERVINGS: 3

A simple breakfasts. This oven-baked omelet is light, fluffy, and perfect for a healthy start to your day.

Ingredients:

- 6 large eggs
- 300 ml unsweetened almond milk
- 1/2 teaspoon salt
- Non-stick cooking spray

Instructions:

1. Prepare the Baking Dish: Preheat your oven to 200°C (390°F). Generously spray the baking dish with non-stick cooking spray to prevent sticking.

2. Mix the Omelet Base: Crack the eggs into a large mixing bowl. Add the almond milk and salt. Whisk the mixture thoroughly until smooth and fully combined. Avoid using a mixer, as it may introduce too much air.

3. Fill the Dish: Pour the egg mixture into the prepared baking dish. Ensure the dish is filled up to 2/3 of its height, leaving room for the omelet to rise while cooking.

4. Bake: Place the dish in the preheated oven and bake for 30 minutes. Do not open the oven during the baking process to maintain the omelet's height and fluffiness.

5. Serve: Once baked, remove the omelet from the oven and let it rest for a minute. Slice into portions and serve immediately.

120 kcal, 14g protein,
4g fat, 3g carbs, 1g fiber

Tips: Serve with fresh herbs, sliced vegetables, or a dollop of non-fat Greek yogurt for added flavor. Use individual ramekins for single servings, adjusting the cooking time slightly if needed.

5. Shakshuka Recipe

PREP: 5 MIN   COOK: 20 MIN   SERVINGS: 2

Shakshuka combines stewed vegetables and poached eggs for a nutrient-packed, satisfying meal. Perfect for breakfast or a light lunch!

Ingredients:

- 3 eggs
- 300 g tomatoes, diced
- 100 g onion, thinly sliced
- 100 ml tomato puree
- 1/2 red bell pepper, thinly sliced
- 10 g garlic, finely chopped
- 1 red chili pepper, thinly sliced
- 1 tbsp sweet paprika
- 1/2 tsp salt
- 1/2 tsp black pepper
- Cooking spray for sautéing
- 5 g fresh parsley, chopped

Instructions:

1. Prepare Vegetables: Dice the tomatoes. Thinly slice the onion and red bell pepper. Finely chop the garlic and slice the red chili.

2. Sauté Aromatics: Heat a skillet over medium heat and lightly coat it with cooking spray. Add garlic and red chili. Sauté for 30 seconds until fragrant.

3. Cook Vegetables: Add the diced tomatoes, onion, and bell pepper to the skillet. Cook for 2 minutes, stirring occasionally.

4. Simmer Sauce: Stir in the tomato puree and reduce the heat to low. Simmer for 10 minutes, allowing the sauce to thicken and flavors to meld.

5. Season: Add sweet paprika, salt, and black pepper. Mix well and cook for another 3 minutes.

6. Add Eggs: Use a spoon or spatula to create small wells in the vegetable mixture. Crack one egg into each well. Cover the skillet and cook on low heat for 4 minutes, or until egg whites are set and yolks are still slightly runny.

7. Garnish and Serve: Sprinkle with fresh parsley before serving. Serve hot, directly in the skillet.

150 kcal, 10g protein, 5g fat, 12g carbs, 4g fiber

Tips: *For extra flavor, use smoked paprika instead of sweet paprika.*
Add dollop of yogurt for a creamy touch.
Adjust the spice level by reducing or omitting the chili pepper.

6. Vegetable Casserole with Zucchini and Spinach

PREP: 5 MIN   COOK: 25 MIN   SERVINGS: 2

Zucchini and spinach are rich in fiber, promoting healthy digestion, while eggs provide a protein boost.

Ingredients:

- 2 eggs
- 1/2 cup chopped zucchini
- 1/2 cup chopped fresh

Instructions:

1. Preheat the Oven: Preheat your oven to 180°C (350°F).

2. Prepare the Baking Dish: Lightly coat a baking dish with cooking spray.

- spinach
- 1/4 cup chopped onion
- Cooking spray
- Pinch of salt and ground pepper

3. Sauté the Vegetables: Heat a skillet over medium heat, spray lightly with cooking spray, and sauté the zucchini and onion for 3-4 minutes until softened.

4. Assemble the Casserole: Transfer the sautéed vegetables to the baking dish and add the spinach.

5. Mix and Pour: In a bowl, whisk the eggs with salt and pepper. Pour the egg mixture evenly over the vegetables.

6. Bake: Bake in the oven for 15 minutes, or until the eggs are set.

7. Serve: Serve hot and enjoy a nutritious start to your day.

150 kcal, 12g protein, 7g fat, 4g carbs, 1g fiber

Tips: Add a hint of garlic or dried thyme to elevate the flavor.

7. Lazy Cottage Cheese Dumplings with Chickpea Flour

PREP: 10 MIN   COOK: 20 MIN   SERVINGS: 2

A simple and tasty meal with light Cottage Cheese Dumplings paired with a refreshing fruit sauce.

Ingredients:

- 180 g low-fat cottage cheese
- 1 large egg
- 3 tablespoons (30 g) chickpea flour
- Pinch of salt
- Fresh strawberries or fruit – for sauce

Instructions:

1. Prepare the Ingredients: Gather all necessary ingredients. Ensure the cottage cheese is smooth and free of large lumps.

2. Mix the Dough: In a mixing bowl, whisk the egg lightly with a fork. Add the cottage cheese and stir until well combined. Gradually incorporate the chickpea flour and mix thoroughly to form a soft dough.

3. Shape the Dumplings: Divide the dough into small portions and roll them into smooth balls. Keep the size small, as they will slightly expand when cooked.

4. Cook the Dumplings: Bring a pot of water to a boil and add a pinch of salt. Carefully drop the dumplings into the boiling water. Cook for 2-3 minutes after they float to the surface.

5. Prepare the Strawberry Sauce: Blend fresh strawberries into a smooth puree using a blender. No added sugar is needed for zero points.

6. Serve: Pour the strawberry sauce over the dumplings.
Serve warm and enjoy this guilt-free, nutritious treat.

120 kcal, 14g protein,
2g fat, 10g carbs, 2g fiber

Tips: Chickpea flour adds a subtle nutty flavor that complements the cottage cheese. Use other zero-point fruits, such as raspberries or blueberries, for variety in the sauce. Add a pinch of cinnamon or vanilla extract to the dough for an extra layer of flavor.

8. Egg White Scramble

PREP: 5 MIN   COOK: 7 MIN   SERVINGS: 2

A light, protein-rich breakfast that's quick and flavorful. Ideal for busy mornings or a healthy meal prep option!

Ingredients:

- 6 large eggs (200 g) egg whites
- 1 cup (30 g) fresh spinach
- 1/2 cup (75 g) cherry tomatoes, halved
- 1/2 cup (50 g) mushrooms, sliced
- 2 stalks (15 g) green onion, chopped
- 1/4 tsp salt (to taste)
- 1/4 tsp black pepper (to taste)
- Cooking spray

Instructions:

1. Prepare the Vegetables: Chop the green onion, slice the mushrooms, and halve the cherry tomatoes.

2. Preheat the Skillet: Spray a nonstick skillet lightly with cooking spray. Heat the skillet over medium heat.

3. Cook the Vegetables: Add the mushrooms to the skillet and sauté for 2-3 minutes until softened. Stir in the cherry tomatoes and spinach. Cook for another 2 minutes until the spinach wilts and the tomatoes soften.

4. Add the Egg Whites: Pour the egg whites into the skillet. Season with salt and black pepper. Stir gently, cooking for 2-3 minutes until the egg whites are set but still moist.

5. Serve: Remove from heat and garnish with chopped green onions.

70 kcal, 14g protein,
0g fat, 3g carbs, 1g fiber

Tips: To keep your egg whites soft and fluffy, remove them from the heat just before they are fully set, as they will continue to cook slightly off the heat.

9. Vegetable Salad with Cucumber, Tomato, and Radish

PREP: 5 MIN   COOK: 5 MIN   SERVINGS: 1

This light salad is packed with vitamins and minerals to support a healthy metabolism.

Ingredients:

- 1/2 cup (50 g) cucumber, sliced
- 1/2 cup (50 g) tomato, chopped
- 1/4 cup (25 g) radish, sliced
- 1 tsp lemon juice
- Pinch of salt and black pepper
- Few sprigs of fresh dill, for garnish

45 kcal, 1g protein, 0g fat, 10g carbs, 2g fiber

Instructions:

1. Combine cucumber, tomato, and radish in a mixing bowl.

2. Drizzle with lemon juice and sprinkle with salt and pepper.

3. Toss gently to mix, and garnish with fresh dill.

4. Serve chilled.

Tips: Add a handful of shredded carrots for a touch of sweetness.

 ## 10. Sweet Black-Eyed Pea Breakfast Porridge

PREP: 5 MIN   COOK: 10 MIN   SERVINGS: 2

A unique, nutritious breakfast combining black-eyed peas and fresh fruits for a creamy, naturally sweet start to your day.

Ingredients:

- 1/2 cup (100 g) cooked black-eyed peas
- 1/2 cup (120 ml) almond milk (unsweetened)
- 1 large banana, mashed
- 1/2 tsp ground cinnamon
- 1/2 tsp vanilla extract
- 1 tbsp sweetener (like Lakanto Monkfruit) or to taste
- 1 tbsp chia seeds (optional, for added texture)
- 1/2 cup (75 g) fresh fruits (berries, mango, or kiwi)

Instructions:

1. Prepare the Base: In a small saucepan, combine the cooked black-eyed peas, almond milk, mashed banana, cinnamon, and vanilla extract. Heat over medium heat, stirring occasionally, until the mixture is warm and creamy (about 5 minutes).

2. Sweeten the Porridge: Stir in the sweetener, adjusting to your desired sweetness.

3. Add Chia Seeds (Optional): For a thicker texture, stir in chia seeds and let the mixture sit for 2-3 minutes to thicken.

4. Assemble the Bowl: Divide the warm porridge between two bowls. Top each with fresh fruits for added color and flavor.

5. Serve: Serve immediately and enjoy this hearty, naturally sweet breakfast.

If Using Dried Black-Eyed Peas: Rinse under cold water, soak for 6-8 hours or overnight. Drain, rinse again, and simmer in fresh water for 30-40 minutes until tender. Drain and set aside.

190 kcal, 8g protein, 2g fat, 32g carbs, 6g fiber

Tips: Add a sprinkle of flaxseed for extra texture and healthy fats.

Berry Parfait with Greek Yogurt

PREP: 5 MIN   COOK: 5 MIN   SERVINGS: 2

A refreshing and simple breakfast or snack, packed with protein and antioxidants from fresh berries.

Ingredients:

- 1 cup (240 g) Greek yogurt (non-fat or low-fat)
- 1/2 cup (75 g) mixed fresh berries:
- 25 g strawberries
- 25 g blueberries
- 25 g raspberries
- Optional: A sprinkle of cinnamon or a drizzle of sugar-free syrup for garnish

Instructions:

1. Create the First Layer: Divide 80 g of Greek yogurt between two small glasses or bowls.
Add 25 g of mixed berries on top of each.

2. Add the Second Layer: Repeat the process, layering the remaining yogurt and berries.

3. Garnish: Top with a few extra berries for presentation.
Sprinkle with cinnamon or drizzle with sugar-free syrup for added flavor, if desired.

90 kcal, 10g protein, 0g fat, 8g carbs, 0g fiber

Tips: *Use frozen berries when fresh ones aren't available—just thaw slightly before layering. Perfect for meal prep: Assemble in jars for a grab-and-go snack.*

12. Pancakes

PREP: 10 MIN   COOK: 30 MIN   SERVINGS: 4

These pancakes are incredibly adaptable—pair them with fresh berries, banana slices, or sugar-free syrup for a sweet start to your day. Or use them as a base for creative sweet toasts topped with yogurt.

Ingredients:

- 240 g chickpea flour
- A pinch of cinnamon
- 1/2 tsp baking soda, activated with vinegar
- 220 ml unsweetened almond milk
- 4 large eggs, separated
- 2 tbsp sugar substitute
- A pinch of salt
- Non-stick cooking spray
- Fresh fruit

Instructions:

1. Prepare the Batter Base: In a large mixing bowl, whisk together the egg yolks, sugar substitute, and cinnamon.
Gradually add almond milk, whisking until smooth.
Sift in chickpea flour and mix well. Add baking soda activated with vinegar and stir to combine.

2. Whip the Egg Whites: In a separate bowl, beat egg whites with a pinch of salt until stiff peaks form.

3. Fold the Mixtures: Gently fold the whipped egg whites into the batter

- Sugar-free syrup or unsweetened yogurt

in portions, using a spatula to preserve the airy texture.

4. Cook the Pancakes: Heat a non-stick skillet over medium heat and lightly coat with cooking spray.
Pour small amounts of batter onto the skillet to form pancakes (about 4 dessert spoons each).
Cook for 1.5-2 minutes until bubbles appear on the surface. Flip and cook for another minute until golden.

5. Repeat: Repeat with remaining batter, reapplying cooking spray as needed.

6. Serve: Stack pancakes and top with fresh fruit, sugar-free syrup, or unsweetened yogurt.

140 kcal, 9g protein, 4g fat, 14g carbs, 3g fiber

Tips: *For extra fluffiness, fold the egg whites into the batter in three small portions. Experiment with toppings like a sprinkle of cocoa powder or a dash of lemon zest for added flavor.*

13. Vegetable Bake with Mushrooms

PREP: 10 MIN   COOK: 20 MIN   SERVINGS: 2

A healthy, protein-packed dish with vegetables, eggs, and mushrooms that provides essential vitamins and keeps you full longer.

Ingredients:

- 2 large eggs
- 1/2 cup (50 g) sliced mushrooms
- 1/4 cup (30 g) chopped onion
- 1/4 cup (40 g) diced tomatoes
- 1/4 cup (40 g) diced bell pepper
- Cooking spray

Instructions:

1. Prepare the Baking Dish: Lightly coat a small baking dish with cooking spray. Preheat your oven to 180°C (350°F).

2. Mix the Eggs: In a bowl, whisk the eggs until smooth.

3. Arrange mushrooms, onion, tomatoes, and bell pepper evenly in the baking dish. Pour the whisked eggs over the vegetables, ensuring they are evenly coated.

4. Bake: Place the dish in the oven and bake for 20 minutes, or until the egg mixture is firm and cooked through.

5. Serve: Remove from the oven and serve warm.

150 kcal, 13g protein, 6g fat, 6g carbs, 2g fiber

Tips: *Swap in vegetables like zucchini or cauliflower for variety. Add fresh herbs like parsley or chives for extra flavor.*

14. Sweet Lentil & Green Pea Breakfast Bowl

PREP: 5 MIN   COOK: 10 MIN   SERVINGS: 2

A unique and wholesome breakfast combining the natural sweetness of banana with the nutritional power of lentils and peas for a fiber-rich and protein-packed start to your day.

Ingredients:

- 100 g (1/2 cup) cooked green lentils
- 80 g (1/2 cup) cooked green peas
- 1 large (120 g) banana, mashed
- 120 ml (1/2 cup) almond milk
- 1/2 tsp cinnamon
- 1/2 tsp vanilla extract
- 1-2 tsp sweetener (to taste)
- 1 tbsp chia seeds (optional)
- 1/2 cup (70 g) mixed fresh fruits (e.g., berries, mango, or kiwi)

Instructions:

1. Prepare the Base: In a small saucepan, combine the cooked lentils, green peas, almond milk, mashed banana, cinnamon, and vanilla extract. Heat over medium-low heat, stirring occasionally, for about 5 minutes until warm and creamy.

2. Add Sweetener: Stir in honey or your preferred sweetener to taste.

3. Thicken (Optional): If using chia seeds, mix them into the warm mixture and let sit for 2-3 minutes for a thicker consistency.

4. Assemble the Bowls: Divide the lentil-pea mixture evenly between two bowls. Top with fresh fruits and sprinkle with nuts or seeds, if desired.

5. Serve: Enjoy warm for a comforting breakfast or chilled as a refreshing summer option.

 200 kcal, 10g protein, 2g fat, 32g carbs, 7g fiber

Tips: *Swap almond milk with oat or soy milk for a different flavor. Try seasonal fruits for topping to keep the dish exciting year-round.*

15. Smoked Salmon Omelette with Creamy Cheese

PREP: 5 MIN   COOK: 10 MIN   SERVINGS: 1

Indulge in the perfect harmony of flavors with this fluffy egg white omelette, featuring delicate slices of smoky salmon and fat-free creamy cheese, complemented by fresh spinach and a hint of seasoning.

Ingredients:

- 3 large egg whites (or 2 whole eggs + 1 white)
- 50 g smoked salmon, thinly sliced
- 2 tbsp fat-free cottage cheese or Greek yogurt

Instructions:

1. Prepare Ingredients: Slice the smoked salmon into small pieces. Chop dill or chives, if desired.

2. Whisk Eggs: In a small bowl, whisk the egg whites (or eggs) with a pinch of salt and pepper until slightly frothy.

- 1/4 cup (30 g) fresh spinach or arugula
- 1 tbsp (3 g) chopped fresh dill or chives (optional)
- Pinch of salt
- Pinch of freshly ground black pepper
- Cooking spray

3. Cook Omelette: Heat a non-stick skillet over medium heat and lightly grease with cooking spray.
Pour the egg mixture into the skillet and tilt to spread evenly. Cook for 2-3 minutes until the base sets but the top remains slightly runny.

4. Add Filling: On one half of the omelette, layer smoked salmon, a few dollops of cottage cheese or Greek yogurt, and spinach or arugula. Sprinkle with dill or chives, if using.

5. Fold and Finish: Gently fold the empty half of the omelette over the filling. Cover the skillet with a lid and cook for another 2-3 minutes to set the eggs fully and warm the filling.

6. Serve: Slide the omelette onto a plate, garnish with extra dill or chives if desired, and serve hot.

160 kcal, 20g protein, 6g fat, 3g carbs, 1g fiber

Tips: For added zest, squeeze fresh lemon juice over the omelette before serving. For a stronger flavor, swap the dill for capers or a pinch of smoked paprika.

16. Banana Pancakes

PREP: 5 MIN   COOK: 10 MIN   SERVINGS: 2

Naturally sweet and fluffy pancakes made with ripe banana and chickpea flour, perfect for a healthy and satisfying breakfast or snack.

Ingredients:

- 1 medium (120 g) banana
- 2 large (100 g) eggs
- 60 g chickpea flour
- 1/3 tsp (1 g) baking powder
- Optional: Sugar substitute (adjust to taste)

Instructions:

1. Prepare Ingredients: Peel the banana and slice it into a mixing bowl. Use a ripe banana for a naturally sweet flavor.

2. Blend the Base: Add the eggs to the banana slices. Blend with an immersion blender until smooth and frothy.

3. Incorporate Dry Ingredients: Add the chickpea flour and baking powder.
Mix thoroughly using a whisk until the batter is smooth and free of lumps.

4. Cook Pancakes: Heat a nonstick skillet over medium heat. Lightly spray with cooking spray if needed.
Spoon about 30 g (2 tablespoons) of batter for each pancake.
Cook for ~2 minutes on the first side, flip, and cook for another minute until golden brown.

5. Serve: Stack the pancakes on a plate. Top with sugar-free syrup, fresh fruit, or enjoy them plain.

160 kcal, 20g protein, 6g fat, 3g carbs, 1g fiber

Tips: Use a very ripe banana for enhanced sweetness and a richer flavor. For extra fluffiness, let the batter rest for 2-3 minutes before cooking.

 ## 17. Cabbage Rolls with Egg

PREP: 7 MIN   COOK: 20 MIN   SERVINGS: 2

A balanced and nutritious breakfast, packed with fiber from cabbage and protein from eggs.

Ingredients:

- 2 large green cabbage leaves
- 2 eggs
- 1/4 cup diced tomato
- 1 tablespoon chopped green onion
- A pinch of salt

Instructions:

1. Boil the cabbage leaves in hot water for 2-3 minutes until they soften.

2. In a bowl, whisk the eggs and mix in the tomatoes, green onion, and a pinch of salt.

3. Cook the egg mixture in a skillet with cooking spray to form an omelet.

4. Wrap the omelet in the cabbage leaves, forming rolls.

5. Serve warm.

130 kcal, 10g protein, 5g fat, 8g carbs, 3g fiber

Tips: Use savoy cabbage leaves for a softer texture.

 ## 18. Airy Cottage Cheese Casserole with Berries

PREP: 10 MIN   COOK: 1 HR   SERVINGS: 5

A light, protein-rich casserole packed with the natural sweetness of berries, perfect for breakfast, dessert, or a wholesome snack.

Ingredients:

- 100 ml unsweetened almond milk
- 450 g low-fat cottage cheese
- 4 eggs

Instructions:

1. Prepare the Base Mixture: In a large bowl, combine low-fat cottage cheese, almond milk, eggs, and sweetener.
Blend the mixture using a hand blender until smooth and creamy.

2. Incorporate the Cornstarch: Gradually add cornstarch to the cottage

- 40 g cornstarch
- Sweetener to taste
- 1/2 cup (75 g) fresh or frozen berries (e.g., blueberries, raspberries, or strawberries)
- Cooking spray (to grease the baking dish)

cheese mixture. Stir thoroughly until the cornstarch is fully incorporated.

3. Prepare the Baking Dish: Lightly grease the baking dish with cooking spray to prevent sticking.
Pour the prepared cottage cheese mixture into the dish, spreading it evenly.

4. Add the Berries: Scatter the fresh or frozen berries over the surface of the mixture.

5. Bake the Casserole: Preheat the oven to 180°C (350°F). Place the baking dish in the oven and bake for approximately 1 hour or until the top is set and golden.

6. Cool Before Serving: Once baked, turn off the oven and let the casserole cool completely inside. This helps prevent it from deflating and ensures a firm texture.

7. Serve and Enjoy: Slice the cooled casserole into portions and serve as a delicious breakfast, snack, or dessert.

120 kcal, 13g protein, 3g fat, 9g carbs, 1g fiber

Tips: Use a mix of berries for a more vibrant flavor and color. For extra sweetness, drizzle with a sugar-free syrup or honey (optional).

 19. Vegetable Omelette with Greens

PREP: 5 MIN   COOK: 10 MIN   SERVINGS: 1

This omelette is rich in protein and fiber, which help maintain stable energy levels and prevent overeating.

Ingredients:

- 3 egg whites
- 1 egg
- 1/2 cup chopped spinach
- 1/4 cup chopped red bell pepper
- 2 tablespoons chopped green onion
- Cooking spray

Instructions:

1. Heat a skillet over medium heat and lightly coat with cooking spray.

2. In a small bowl, whisk the egg whites and whole egg until well combined.

3. Add the chopped spinach, bell pepper, and green onion.

4. Pour the mixture into the skillet and cook for 3-4 minutes until the edges begin to set.

5. Carefully flip the omelette with a spatula and cook for another 2 minutes. Serve hot.

120 kcal, 14g protein,
4g fat, 3g carbs, 1g fiber

Tips: *For extra flavor, add a pinch of garlic powder or smoked paprika.*
You can use any other greens like kale or arugula instead of spinach for variety.

 20. # Pumpkin Spice Bread or Muffins

PREP: 10 MIN   COOK: 45 MIN   SERVINGS: 1-12

A healthy and flavorful Pumpkin Spice Bread recipe perfect for breakfast, snacks, or dessert.

Ingredients:

- 1/2 cups self-rising flour (or chickpea flour for added protein and fiber)
- 1 tsp baking powder
- 1 tsp baking soda
- 2 tsp ground cinnamon
- 1/4 tsp ground nutmeg
- 1/4 tsp ground cloves
- 1 egg or 2 egg whites
- 1 tsp vanilla extract
- 1/2 cup granulated sugar substitute (Lakanto Classic Monkfruit Sweetener or similar)
- 1/2 cup brown sugar substitute (Lakanto Golden Monkfruit Sweetener or similar)
- 2 cups pumpkin purée (unsweetened)
- 2 Tbsp unsweetened applesauce

Instructions:

1. Preheat Oven: Set your oven to 350°F (175°C). Prepare a 9x5 bread pan or 12-cup muffin tin by spraying it lightly with nonstick cooking spray.

2. Mix Dry Ingredients: In a large mixing bowl, combine the flour, baking powder, baking soda, cinnamon, nutmeg, and cloves. Whisk well to evenly distribute the spices.

3. Prepare Wet Ingredients: In another bowl, whisk together the egg (or egg whites), vanilla extract, granulated sugar substitute, brown sugar substitute, and pumpkin purée until smooth.

4. Combine Wet and Dry: Gradually pour the wet mixture into the dry ingredients while stirring gently.
Add the unsweetened applesauce and stir until just combined. Do not overmix, as this can affect the texture.

5. Bake: Pour the batter into the prepared loaf pan or muffin tin.
Bake for 40–45 minutes for the loaf or 15–18 minutes for muffins, or until a toothpick inserted in the center comes out clean.

6. Cool: Let the bread or muffins cool for 5 minutes before removing them from the pan.

90 kcal, 3g protein,
1g fat, 15g carbs, 3g fiber

Tips: *Substitute the applesauce with mashed bananas for a different flavor twist.*

Start your day with a nutritious and satisfying breakfast to ensure you have plenty of energy to tackle the day ahead. Consider adding a variety of greens, vegetables, and fruits to your plate for an extra boost of vitamins and fiber. Experiment with different flavor combinations and textures to keep your breakfasts exciting and enjoyable. A well-balanced breakfast sets the tone for healthier choices throughout the day, so make it count!

21. Zucchini Manicotti

PREP: 20 MIN   COOK: 30 MIN   SERVINGS: 4

This lighter version of manicotti uses thin zucchini slices in place of pasta, with a flavorful zero-point filling made from cottage cheese and spinach. Perfect for a guilt-free, satisfying meal!

Ingredients:

- 2 medium zucchinis (200 g each)
- 200 g fat-free cottage cheese (zero-point alternative to ricotta)
- 225 g frozen spinach, thawed and thoroughly squeezed dry
- Salt and pepper to taste
- 1/2 yellow onion (75 g), finely diced
- 3 cloves garlic, minced (10 g)
- 1 can (400 g) crushed tomatoes (preferably no-salt-added)
- 1 teaspoon dried basil (or 2 tablespoons fresh, minced)
- 1 teaspoon dried oregano
- Salt and pepper to taste

Instructions:

1. Prepare the Marinara Sauce: In a medium saucepan, heat a non-stick skillet over medium heat. Add the diced onion and minced garlic. Sauté for about 5 minutes until the onion is translucent and the garlic is fragrant. Add the crushed tomatoes, dried basil, and oregano, stirring to combine. Season with salt and pepper to taste, then let the sauce simmer for about 10 minutes. Set aside.

2. Prepare the Filling: In a bowl, combine the cottage cheese with the thawed spinach. Add a pinch of salt and pepper and stir until well mixed.

3. Slice the Zucchini: Preheat the oven to 400°F (200°C). Using a mandoline or vegetable peeler, slice the zucchini lengthwise into long, thin strips.

4. Assemble the Rolls: Lay two zucchini strips side by side, overlapping slightly. Place about 2 tablespoons of the cottage cheese and spinach filling at one end of the strips, then roll up the zucchini around the filling. Place each roll seam-side down in a baking dish with half of the marinara sauce spread on the bottom. Repeat with remaining zucchini and filling.

5. Bake: Cover the dish with foil and bake for 25-30 minutes, until the rolls are tender and the sauce is bubbling.

6. Serve: Remove from the oven and let cool for a few minutes. Top with fresh basil, if desired, and serve with extra marinara sauce on the side.

100 kcal, 10g protein, 2g fat, 12g carbs, 4g fiber

Tips: When the zucchini core becomes too seedy, set it aside for another use and start with a new zucchini if needed.

22. ## BBQ Slow Cooker Chicken

PREP: 5 MIN   COOK: 4-6 HR   SERVINGS: 4

This zero-point BBQ chicken is perfect for meal prep, potlucks, or any day you're craving a low-carb, delicious dinner. With minimal ingredients and a slow cooker, you'll have tender, flavorful BBQ chicken that everyone will love!

Ingredients:

- 2 lbs (1 kg) boneless, skinless chicken breasts
- 1 cup sugar-free BBQ sauce (I recommend G Hughes Sugar Free Hickory BBQ Sauce)
- 1 tbsp brown sugar substitute (Lakanto Golden Monkfruit Sweetener works well)
- 1 tsp Worcestershire sauce
- Salt, to taste

140 kcal, 29g protein, 4g fat, 3g carbs, 0g fiber

Instructions:

1. Season the Chicken: Sprinkle salt over the chicken breasts and place them in the slow cooker.

2. Prepare the Sauce: In a small bowl, whisk together the BBQ sauce, Worcestershire sauce, and brown sugar substitute until smooth.

3. Add Sauce to the Slow Cooker: Pour the sauce over the chicken, making sure each piece is coated. Cover with the lid.

4. Cook the Chicken: Set the slow cooker to low and cook for 4–6 hours until the chicken is tender.

5. Shred the Chicken: Remove the lid and, using two forks, shred the chicken directly in the slow cooker. Stir to mix the chicken with the sauce.

6. Finish and Serve: Let the shredded chicken sit in the sauce for another 20 minutes on low to absorb the flavors fully. Serve salad or other side dishes

Tips: If you prefer a slightly sweeter BBQ, add a bit more brown sugar substitute to the sauce. This BBQ chicken is delicious on its own, with a low-calorie coleslaw

 23. ## Cilantro Lime Cauliflower Rice

PREP: 5 MIN   COOK: 5 MIN   SERVINGS: 2

A fresh and tangy zero-point side dish inspired by Mexican flavors, perfect for burrito bowls, tacos, or as a zesty companion to your favorite meals.

Ingredients:

- 1 large head of cauliflower (600 g), riced
- 2 garlic cloves (10 g), minced
- 1 bunch fresh cilantro (30 g), finely chopped
- Juice and zest of 2 small limes (30 ml juice)
- Salt and pepper to taste
- 1/2 tsp (2.5 ml) olive oil (optional, for skillet)

Instructions:

1. Rice the Cauliflower: Remove the leaves and core from the cauliflower. Cut into florets and pulse in a food processor until the texture resembles rice.

2. Heat the Skillet: Lightly coat a large skillet with olive oil (optional) and heat over medium heat.

3. Cook Garlic and Cauliflower: Add minced garlic to the skillet and sauté for about 1 minute until fragrant.
Stir in the cauliflower rice, lime zest, and lime juice. Cook for 5 minutes, stirring often, until the cauliflower is tender but still slightly crisp.

4. Add Cilantro: Remove the skillet from heat. Fold in the chopped cilantro and season with salt and pepper to taste.

5. Serve: Garnish with extra cilantro or lime wedges, if desired. Serve warm.

35 kcal, 2g protein, 0.5g fat, 6g carbs, 2g fiber

Tips: Avoid overcooking to keep the cauliflower rice from getting mushy. Lime zest adds brightness and depth, enhancing the flavor. Customize the Seasoning: For a spicy kick, try adding a pinch of cumin or chili powder.

 ## 24. Stewed Vegetables with Chicken in Yogurt Sauce

PREP: 10 MIN   COOK: 35 MIN   SERVINGS: 3

The chicken provides protein, while the vegetables and light coconut sauce contain fiber and healthy fats to keep you energized and feeling satiated.

Ingredients:

- 150 g chicken breast cubed
- 1 medium zucchini (200 g) cubed
- 1 medium carrot (100 g) sliced
- 200 g broccoli florets
- 200 ml non-fat plain yogurt
- 2 cloves garlic (10 g) minced
- 1 tsp fresh ginger (5 g) grated

Instructions:

1. Prepare the Chicken: Slice the chicken breast into bite-sized cubes. Marinate the chicken in lime juice, soy sauce, and a pinch of grated ginger for 10 minutes while preparing the vegetables.

2. Cook the Chicken: Heat a skillet or wok on medium heat, coat with cooking spray, and sear the chicken pieces until lightly browned. Remove from the skillet and set aside.

3. Sauté the Vegetables: In the same skillet, add garlic and the remaining ginger. Sauté until aromatic, about 1 minute. Add the carrots and broccoli first (as they take longer to cook) and stir-fry for 5 minutes. Add zucchini and cook for an additional 3 minutes until the vegetables are tender but

- 1 tbsp low-sodium soy sauce (15 ml)
- 1 tbsp lime juice (15 ml)
- Fresh cilantro or parsley chopped
- Salt to taste
- Pepper to taste
- Cooking spray

still crisp.

4. Combine Chicken and Sauce: Return the chicken to the skillet. Lower the heat and stir in the yogurt. Season with salt and pepper to taste. Simmer for 5-7 minutes, stirring occasionally, to let the flavors meld together.

5. Garnish and Serve: Sprinkle fresh cilantro or parsley over the dish for a burst of color and flavor. Serve warm, either on its own or with a side of cauliflower rice or spiralized vegetable

220 kcal, 30g protein, 5g fat, 10g carbs, 4g fiber

Tips: *Use turkey breast instead of chicken for variety.*
Add a pinch of chili flakes for a spicy kick.

25. Vegetable Stir Fry

PREP: 5 MIN   COOK: 10 MIN   SERVINGS: 6

This vibrant, healthy vegetable stir fry features a mix of colorful veggies coated in a savory, zero-point sauce. It's oil-free, quick, and perfect as a side or light main dish.

Ingredients:

- 1 red bell pepper (100 g) sliced
- 1 yellow bell pepper (100 g) sliced
- 1 cup sugar snap peas (120 g)
- 1 cup carrots (130 g) sliced
- 1 cup mushrooms (100 g) sliced
- 2 cups broccoli florets (200 g)
- 1 cup baby corn (150 g) drained and chopped if whole
- 1/2 cup water chestnuts (75 g, sliced
- 1/4 cup low-sodium soy sauce (60 ml)
- 3 garlic cloves (9 g)minced
- 1 tsp fresh ginger (5 g) minced (optional)
- 1/2 cup vegetable or chicken broth (120 ml)

Instructions:

1. Cook the Vegetables: Heat a wok or large skillet over medium-high heat. Add a splash of broth. Add the bell peppers, sugar snap peas, carrots, mushrooms, broccoli, baby corn, and water chestnuts. Stir-fry for 2–3 minutes until the vegetables are slightly tender.

2. Make the Sauce: In a small bowl, whisk together the soy sauce, garlic, ginger, remaining broth, and cornstarch mixture until smooth.

3. Combine and Cook: Pour the sauce over the vegetables in the skillet. Cook for an additional 1–2 minutes, stirring constantly, until the sauce thickens and coats the vegetables evenly.

4. Serve: Transfer to a serving dish. Garnish with green onions and sesame seeds, if desired.

- 1 tbsp cornstarch, dissolved in 2 tbsp water
- Chopped green onions and sesame seeds for garnish (optional)

40 kcal, 2g protein, 0g fat, 8g carbs, 3g fiber

Tips: Customize Your Veggies: Swap in other vegetables like zucchini, cauliflower, or bok choy based on availability or preference. Spicy Option: Add red chili flakes or sriracha for a spicy kick.
Pairing Idea: Serve with cauliflower rice or zucchini noodles for a complete meal.

26. Turkey in Tomato-Basil Sauce

PREP: 10 MIN   COOK: 35 MIN   SERVINGS: 3

Turkey is high in protein, promoting muscle recovery and prolonged satiety, while tomatoes and basil provide vitamins and antioxidants.

Ingredients:

- 150 g turkey fillet cubed
- 3 tomatoes (360 g) diced
- 1 onion (150 g) sliced
- 2 cloves garlic (10 g) minced
- 1 tbsp basil chopped or dried
- Cooking spray
- Salt to taste
- Pepper to taste

Instructions:

1. Cut the turkey into small cubes, dice the tomatoes, and slice the onion into half-rings.

2. Heat a skillet over medium heat, lightly coat with cooking spray, and sauté the turkey for 6–7 minutes until golden brown. Set aside.

3. In the same skillet, sauté the onion and garlic until softened.

4. Add the tomatoes and basil, then simmer over low heat for 10 minutes.

5. Return the turkey to the skillet, stir to coat with the sauce, and cook for an additional 5 minutes.

200 kcal, 32g protein, 3g fat, 7g carbs, 2g fiber

Tips: Add spinach for extra nutrients or substitute turkey with chicken.

27. Fish & Chips

PREP: 10 MIN   COOK: 25 MIN   SERVINGS: 3

This healthier take on the classic Fish & Chips swaps heavy batter and deep frying for baked, flavorful alternatives. A guilt-free, satisfying meal

Ingredients:

- **For the Fish:**
- 1 lb (450g) white fish fillets (cod, haddock, or pollock)
- 1 egg white, lightly beaten
- 1/2 cup (50g) chickpea flour (or almond flour for zero points)
- 1/2 teaspoon garlic powder
- 1/2 teaspoon smoked paprika
- Salt and pepper, to taste
- **For the Chips:**
- 2 medium zucchinis or carrots, cut into thin wedges or sticks
- 1 teaspoon smoked paprika or garlic powder
- 1 teaspoon lemon zest (optional)
- Salt and pepper, to taste
- **For the Dipping Sauce:**
- 1/2 cup (120g) non-fat Greek yogurt
- 1 tablespoon Dijon mustard
- 1 teaspoon lemon juice
- 1 teaspoon fresh dill or parsley, chopped
- Salt and pepper, to taste

Instructions:

1. Preheat the Oven: Preheat your oven to 425°F (220°C). Line a large baking sheet with parchment paper or a silicone baking mat.

2. Prepare the Chips: Toss the zucchini or carrot sticks with your chosen seasonings (smoked paprika, garlic powder, salt, pepper, and lemon zest). Arrange them in a single layer on one side of the baking sheet.

3. Coat the Fish: In a small bowl, whisk the chickpea flour (or almond flour), garlic powder, paprika, salt, and pepper.
Pat the fish fillets dry with a paper towel.
Dip each fish fillet into the egg white, then coat thoroughly in the flour mixture.
Place the coated fish fillets on the other side of the baking sheet.

4. Bake: Spray both the fish and chips lightly with a zero-calorie cooking spray (optional).
Bake for 20-25 minutes, flipping the chips and fish halfway through. The fish should flake easily with a fork, and the chips should be golden and tender.

5. Make the Dipping Sauce: In a small bowl, mix the Greek yogurt, Dijon mustard, lemon juice, fresh dill, salt, and pepper until smooth.
Chill in the refrigerator until ready to serve.

6. Serve: Arrange the baked fish and chips on a plate. Serve with the yogurt-based dipping sauce for a refreshing and tangy flavor.

215 kcal, 42g protein, 3g fat, 17g carbs, 3g fiber

Tips: Use an air fryer for extra crispiness without additional points.
Add a squeeze of lemon juice over the fish and chips before serving for extra zest.

28. Classic Ratatouille

PREP: 20 MIN   COOK: 50 MIN   SERVINGS: 6

A vibrant and oil-free twist on the Mediterranean classic, this ratatouille is bursting with flavors from fresh vegetables and aromatic herbs. Perfect as a side or main dish, it's as delicious as it is healthy.

Ingredients:

- 300 g eggplant
- 300 g zucchini

Instructions:

1. Prepare the Vegetables: Trim the ends of the zucchini and eggplant.
Blanch half of the tomatoes (500 g) in boiling water, peel, and dice them.

- 1 kg tomatoes (500 g for sauce, 500 g for slices)
- 2 onions (150 g), diced
- 2 bell peppers (300 g), diced
- 3 garlic cloves (10 g), minced
- 1 tsp salt
- 1/2 tsp dried oregano
- 1 tsp paprika
- 1/2 tsp dried basil

Dice the bell peppers, onions, and mince the garlic.

2. Make the Sauce: Add a splash of water to a large skillet and sauté the diced onions over medium heat until soft.
Add the diced tomatoes, bell peppers, and half the minced garlic. Cook for 10–15 minutes until the mixture thickens into a sauce.

3. Slice the Vegetables: Slice the zucchini, eggplant, and the remaining tomatoes into rounds about 5 mm thick.

4. Prepare the Herb Mix: In a small bowl, combine the remaining garlic with oregano, paprika, and basil.

5. Assemble the Ratatouille: Spread the tomato and pepper sauce evenly across the bottom of a baking dish.
Layer the zucchini, eggplant, and tomato slices in an alternating pattern over the sauce. Sprinkle with salt and distribute the herb mixture evenly over the vegetables.

6. Bake: Cover the baking dish with foil and bake in a preheated oven at 180°C (350°F) for 30 minutes.
Remove the foil and bake for another 20–25 minutes, until the vegetables are tender and slightly caramelized.

85 kcal, 3g protein, 0.5g fat, 18g carbs, 5g fiber

Tips: *You can also chop the vegetables into small pieces for a quicker version and cook everything together in the skillet with the sauce.*

29. Chicken Fritters

PREP: 15 MIN   COOK: 20 MIN   SERVINGS: 4

These light and juicy chicken fritters are made without flour and use Greek yogurt for added creaminess. A healthier twist on the classic recipe, perfect for any meal or snack!

Ingredients:

- 500–600 g chicken breast fillet, finely chopped
- 30 g green onion, finely chopped
- 30 g parsley, finely chopped
- 100 g hard cheese, grated
- 100 g Greek yogurt
- 2 large eggs
- Salt, to taste

Instructions:

1. Prepare Ingredients: Finely dice the chicken breast. Grate the cheese and chop the green onions and parsley.

2. Mix Wet Ingredients: In a bowl, whisk together the Greek yogurt and eggs. Season with salt and black pepper to taste. Mix until smooth.

3. Combine Ingredients: In a large mixing bowl, combine the chopped chicken, grated cheese, and herbs. Add the yogurt-egg mixture and stir well until all ingredients are evenly incorporated.

- Ground black pepper, to taste
- Vegetable oil, minimal (for greasing the skillet)

4. Let the Mixture Rest: Allow the batter to rest for about 10 minutes to slightly thicken and let the flavors meld together.

5. Cook the Fritters: Heat a nonstick skillet over medium heat and lightly grease it with a small amount of vegetable oil.
Spoon 1-1.5 tablespoons of the mixture into the skillet for each fritter. Flatten slightly with the back of the spoon.

6. Fry:
Cook the fritters for about 3 minutes on each side, or until golden brown and the chicken is fully cooked. Avoid overcrowding the skillet to ensure even cooking.

7. Serve: Remove the fritters from the skillet and let them rest briefly on a paper towel to remove any excess oil. Serve warm or cold.

180 kcal, 25g protein, 7g fat, 3g carbs, 0g fiber

Tips: For a lighter option, bake the fritters at 180°C (350°F) on parchment paper for 15–20 minutes, flipping halfway through. Pair with a refreshing salad or a yogurt-based dipping sauce for extra flavor

 30. Spaghetti Squash

PREP: 5 MIN   COOK: 30-40 MIN   SERVINGS: 2-4

Spaghetti squash is a versatile and healthy alternative to pasta, offering a naturally low-calorie, nutrient-packed base for your favorite sauces and toppings.

Ingredients:

- 1 spaghetti squash (approximately 800–1,000 g)
- Salt, to taste
- Freshly ground black pepper, to taste

Instructions:

1. Preheat the Oven: Preheat your oven to 400°F (200°C).

2. Prepare the Squash: Using a sharp knife, slice the spaghetti squash in half lengthwise. If the squash is too hard to cut, you can soften it slightly by microwaving it for 1 minute or by baking it whole for 10 minutes before slicing.

3. Remove the Seeds: Use a spoon to scoop out the seeds and any fibrous strands from the center of each half.

4. Season the Squash: Lightly sprinkle salt and pepper on the inside of each half to enhance the flavor.

5. Roast the Squash: Place the squash halves cut side down on a baking sheet lined with parchment paper. Use a fork to poke a few holes in the skin to allow steam to escape while cooking.

6. Bake: Roast for 30-40 minutes. The squash should be fork-tender but slightly firm to maintain a noodle-like texture. Adjust the cooking time depending on the size of the squash.

7. Create the «Spaghetti» Strands: Once the squash is cool enough to handle, use a fork to scrape and fluff the strands, working from the outer edge toward the center.

8. Serve: Season with additional salt and pepper if desired, or use the prepared spaghetti squash in your favorite recipes.

40 kcal, 1g protein, 0g fat, 10g carbs, 2g fiber

Tips: Enhance the flavor by adding garlic powder, Italian herbs, or chili flakes before roasting.

 ## 31. Vegetable Salad with Chicken Breast & Lemon Dressing

PREP: 10 MIN   COOK: 20 MIN   SERVINGS: 1-2

This salad is rich in vitamins, minerals, and protein, helping to boost energy levels and support muscle recovery.

Ingredients:

- 150 g chicken breast sliced
- 1 cucumber (200 g) sliced
- 100 g cherry tomatoes halved
- 100 g lettuce leaves torn
- 5 radishes (50 g) sliced
- 1 tbsp lemon juice (15 ml)
- 1 clove garlic (5 g) grated
- 1 tsp Dijon mustard (5 g)
- Salt to taste
- Pepper to taste

Instructions:

1. Slice the chicken breast (boiled or grilled) into thin strips, cut the cucumber and radishes into rounds, and halve the cherry tomatoes.

2. Tear the lettuce leaves into bite-sized pieces by hand.

3. Prepare the dressing: combine lemon juice, grated garlic, Dijon mustard, salt, and pepper in a small bowl.

4. Combine all ingredients in a large bowl, pour the dressing over, and gently toss to coat evenly.

180 kcal, 30g protein, 2g fat, 8g carbs, 3g fiber

Tips: You can add green onions or substitute turkey for the chicken.

32. Chicken Meatballs with Gravy & Pumpkin Puree

PREP: 15 MIN   COOK: 25 MIN   SERVINGS: 4

This comforting dish pairs tender chicken meatballs with a savory gravy and creamy pumpkin puree, perfect for a wholesome meal.

Ingredients:

- **For the Chicken Meatballs:**
- 400 g ground chicken
- 1 small onion, finely chopped (70 g)
- 1 clove garlic (5 g) minced
- 2 tbsp chopped fresh parsley (10 g)
- 1 egg
- 2 tbsp breadcrumbs (15 g) or ground oats for a lighter option
- 1/2 tsp smoked paprika
- 1/2 tsp dried thyme
- Salt and pepper, to taste
- Cooking spray or 1 tsp olive oil for frying
- **For the Gravy:**
- 1 small onion, finely chopped (70 g)
- 1 clove garlic (5 g) minced
- 250 ml chicken or vegetable broth (low-sodium)
- 1 tsp cornstarch mixed with 2 tbsp cold water
- 1 tsp soy sauce (low-sodium)
- 1/4 tsp black pepper
- 1/4 tsp dried thyme
- **For the Pumpkin Puree:**
- 500 g pumpkin, peeled and cubed
- 120 ml unsweetened almond milk or vegetable broth
- 1/4 tsp nutmeg
- Salt, to taste

Instructions:

1. Prepare the Meatballs: Combine the ground chicken, onion, garlic, parsley, egg, breadcrumbs, smoked paprika, thyme, salt, and pepper in a mixing bowl. Mix well until combined.
Form small meatballs, about 2-3 cm in diameter.
Heat a nonstick skillet over medium heat, lightly greased with cooking spray or olive oil. Fry the meatballs for 6-8 minutes, turning occasionally, until golden brown on all sides. Set aside.

2. Make the Gravy: In the same skillet, sauté the onion and garlic over medium heat until softened, about 3 minutes.
Stir in the broth, soy sauce, thyme, and pepper. Bring to a gentle simmer.
Add the cornstarch slurry and stir until the gravy thickens, about 2-3 minutes.
Return the meatballs to the skillet, spoon the gravy over them, and simmer for another 5 minutes to meld flavors.

3. Prepare the Pumpkin Puree: Steam or boil the pumpkin cubes until tender, about 15 minutes. Drain well.
Mash the pumpkin with almond milk or vegetable broth, nutmeg, and a pinch of salt until smooth. Adjust the consistency by adding more liquid, if needed.

4. Serve: Spoon the pumpkin puree onto plates.
Arrange the meatballs on top and drizzle with gravy.
Garnish with fresh parsley, if desired.

280 kcal, 23g protein, 10g fat, 18g carbs, 4g fiber

Tips: For a creamier gravy, stir in 1 tbsp of Greek yogurt after thickening. Replace pumpkin with butternut squash for a twist.

 ## 33. Tofu Stir-Fry with Vegetables

PREP: 10 MIN+ 30 MIN (MARINATING)   COOK: 10 MIN   SERVINGS: 4

This healthy, plant-based dish features marinated tofu stir-fried with fresh vegetables and sesame for a flavorful and protein-packed meal. Perfect for those following a low-calorie, high-protein diet!

Ingredients:

- **Main Ingredients:**
- 450 g tofu, cut into cubes
- 450 g green peas
- 1 bell pepper (150 g), sliced
- 1 red onion (150 g), sliced
- 1 tsp soy sauce
- 2 tbsp chili sauce
- 1 tsp cornstarch
- 1/3 tsp salt
- 1 tsp water (for cornstarch mixture)
- 2 tbsp sesame seeds (for garnish)
- **Marinade:**
- 3 tbsp soy sauce
- 2 tbsp apple cider vinegar
- 1 garlic clove (5 g), minced
- 1/4 tsp ground chili pepper

Instructions:

1. Marinate the Tofu: In a small bowl, mix the soy sauce, apple cider vinegar, minced garlic, and ground chili pepper to prepare the marinade. Add the tofu cubes to a large bowl, pour the marinade over them, and toss to coat. Let the tofu marinate for 30 minutes.

2. Blanch the Vegetables: Boil salted water in a pot. Add the green peas and blanch for 3 minutes. Drain and rinse under cold water. Slice the bell pepper and onion into thin strips.

3. Cook the Tofu: In a non-stick skillet over medium heat, grill the marinated tofu for about 4 minutes on each side until golden and slightly crispy. Remove and set aside.

4. Prepare the Sauce: In a small bowl, mix the cornstarch with 1 tsp of cold water to create a slurry.

5. Stir-Fry the Vegetables: In the same skillet, add the peas, bell pepper, and onion. Cook over medium heat for 2 minutes.
Add the soy sauce, chili sauce, and cornstarch mixture. Stir for 2–3 minutes until the sauce thickens and coats the vegetables.

6. Assemble the Dish: Serve the vegetables on plates. Top with the grilled tofu cubes. Sprinkle sesame seeds over each portion for garnish.

160 kcal, 12g protein, 5g fat, 16g carbs, 4g fiber

Tips: Extra Crunch: For a crispier tofu texture, coat the tofu cubes in cornstarch before grilling. Add Variety: Substitute or add broccoli, snap peas, or mushrooms for extra flavor and nutrients.

34. Braised Cabbage, Asparagus, Tomato Paste & Turkey

PREP: 10 MIN   COOK: 25 MIN   SERVINGS: 4

A hearty and nutritious dish that combines tender cabbage, crisp asparagus, and flavorful ground turkey in a rich tomato-based sauce.

Ingredients:

- 400 g ground turkey
- 500 g cabbage, thinly

Instructions:

1. Prepare the Ingredients: Thinly slice the cabbage and chop the asparagus. Dice the tomatoes and finely chop the onion and garlic.

- sliced
- 200 g asparagus, trimmed and cut into 4 cm pieces
- 2 tbsp tomato paste
- 2 medium tomatoes (200 g), diced
- 1 medium onion (100 g), finely chopped
- 2 cloves garlic (10 g), minced
- 1 tbsp olive oil or cooking spray
- 120 ml chicken or vegetable broth
- 1 tsp smoked paprika
- 1 tsp dried thyme
- Salt and black pepper, to taste
- Fresh parsley, for garnish (optional)

2. Cook the Ground Turkey:*Heat a large skillet or deep pan over medium heat. Add olive oil or cooking spray.
Sauté the onion and garlic until fragrant, about 2-3 minutes.
Add the ground turkey, breaking it up with a spatula. Cook until browned, about 5-6 minutes. Season with smoked paprika, thyme, salt, and pepper. Remove from the skillet and set aside.

3. Cook the Vegetables: In the same skillet, add the cabbage and cook for 5 minutes, stirring occasionally, until it starts to soften.
Stir in the asparagus and cook for another 3-4 minutes.

4. Add the Tomato Paste and Sauce: Add the tomato paste, diced tomatoes, and broth to the skillet. Stir to coat the vegetables evenly. Return the cooked turkey to the skillet and mix well. Cover and simmer on low heat for 10 minutes (It may require additional cooking time to ensure the cabbage becomes tender and soft, as the desired texture should not be firm), stirring occasionally, until the vegetables are tender and the flavors are well combined.

5. Adjust Seasoning and Serve: Taste and adjust seasoning with additional salt or pepper if needed.
Garnish with fresh parsley, if desired, and serve warm.

220 kcal, 25g protein, 8g fat, 10g carbs, 4g fiber

Tips: Add a pinch of red pepper flakes or chili powder for a kick of heat.

35. Cod Stewed in Tomato Sauce

PREP: 15 MIN   COOK: 25 MIN   SERVINGS: 5

A wholesome and flavorful dish featuring tender cod fillets stewed in a rich tomato sauce, complemented by the sweetness of prunes and the aroma of rosemary. This oil-free recipe is perfect for a balanced, healthy meal.

Ingredients:

- 1.2 kg cod fillets, cut into pieces
- 300 g prunes, soaked and chopped
- 4 sprigs rosemary
- 200 ml water
- 2 tbsp balsamic vinegar
- 1 kg canned tomatoes or tomato puree
- 1 onion (100 g), sliced into

Instructions:

1. Prepare the Prunes: Soak the prunes in warm water for 10–15 minutes. Drain and chop into small pieces.

2. Slice the Onion: Slice the onion into thin half rings.

3. Make the Tomato Sauce: Blend the canned tomatoes in a blender to create a smooth puree, or use pre-made tomato puree.

4. Season the Cod: Cut the cod fillets into pieces and season lightly with

- half rings
- 1/3 tsp salt
- 1/4 tsp ground black pepper

salt and pepper.

5. Cook the Onion: Heat a large skillet over medium heat. Add the sliced onion and a splash of water to prevent sticking. Sauté for about 5–6 minutes until the onion is translucent, adding water as needed.

6. Add the Sauce Ingredients: Stir in the balsamic vinegar and cook for 30 seconds. Add the tomato puree and 200 ml of water. Stir to combine and bring to a gentle boil.

7. Stew the Cod: Add the cod pieces, chopped prunes, and rosemary sprigs to the skillet. Cover with a lid and simmer on low heat for 10–15 minutes until the cod is cooked through and tender.

8. Serve: Remove the rosemary sprigs before serving. Pair with a side of rice, potatoes, or steamed vegetables for a complete meal.

190 kcal, 28g protein, 1g fat, 15g carbs, 4g fiber

Tips: Prune Sweetness: Adjust the amount of prunes based on your desired level of sweetness. Tomato Consistency: For a chunkier sauce, skip blending the canned tomatoes and use them as-is.

36. Chicken Wrapped in Cabbage Leaves

PREP: 10 MIN   COOK: 15 MIN   SERVINGS: 2

This light and nutritious dish features tender chicken breast fillets wrapped in cabbage leaves for a wholesome and flavorful meal. Perfect for a quick, healthy lunch amd dinner!

Ingredients:

- 300 g chicken breast fillets (2 pieces)
- 4 large cabbage leaves
- 1/2 tsp garlic powder
- 1/2 tsp paprika
- Salt and pepper, to taste
- Olive oil spray, for greasing the pan
- Optional garnish: fresh parsley

Instructions:

1. Prepare the Chicken: Place each piece of chicken between two sheets of plastic wrap. Using a meat mallet or rolling pin, gently pound the fillets until they are thin and even.
If the chicken fillets are large, slice them horizontally into two thinner pieces. This will make it easier to pound and ensure even cooking.
Season both sides of the chicken with garlic powder, paprika, salt, and pepper.

2. Blanch the Cabbage Leaves: Bring a pot of water to boil. Blanch the cabbage leaves for 1-2 minutes until they are soft and pliable. Remove and pat dry with a paper towel.

3. Wrap the Chicken: Place each seasoned chicken fillet onto a blanched cabbage leaf. Fold the sides of the leaf over the chicken and roll it tightly to enclose the fillet completely. (something like a taco)

4. Cook the Wrapped Chicken: Heat a non-stick skillet over medium heat and lightly grease it with olive oil spray.
Place the cabbage-wrapped chicken. Cover with a lid and cook for 10-12 minutes, flipping halfway, until the chicken is fully cooked and the cabbage is lightly browned in spots.

5. Serve: Transfer the cooked rolls to a serving plate. Garnish with freshly chopped parsley if desired. Serve hot.

190 kcal, 28g protein, 4g fat, 5g carbs, 2g fiber

Tips: For Extra Flavor: Add a sprinkle of smoked paprika or chili flakes for a spicier version. Alternative Serving: Drizzle with a light tomato sauce or serve with steamed vegetables for a balanced meal.

37. Fish Meatballs with Cauliflower Mash

PREP: 15 MIN   COOK: 20 MIN   SERVINGS: 4

A light and healthy meal featuring tender fish meatballs and creamy cauliflower mash— packed with protein and fiber.

Ingredients:

- **For the Fish Meatballs:**
- 400 g hake or pollock fillet, boneless
- 1 small onion, finely chopped
- 1 clove garlic, minced
- 1/4 cup (30 g) breadcrumbs or ground oats
- 1 egg
- 1 tbsp fresh dill or parsley, chopped
- Pinch of salt
- Pinch of black pepper
- Cooking spray or 1 tsp olive oil
- **For the Cauliflower Mash:**
- 1 medium cauliflower head (~600 g), cut into florets
- 1/4 cup (60 ml) unsweetened almond milk or 1/2 cup (100 ml) non-fat Greek yogurt
- 1 tbsp olive oil
- Pinch of salt

Instructions:

Make the Fish Meatballs:

1. Prepare the Fish Mixture: Blend the fish fillet in a food processor until finely minced, or chop it finely with a knife. In a mixing bowl, combine the minced fish, onion, garlic, breadcrumbs, egg, dill (or parsley), salt, and black pepper. Mix well until evenly combined.

2. Shape the Meatballs: Form the mixture into small meatballs, about 2.5 cm (1 inch) in diameter. You should get 12-16 meatballs.

3. Cook the Meatballs: Heat a nonstick skillet over medium heat and coat with cooking spray or olive oil.
Cook the meatballs for 3-4 minutes per side, until golden brown and cooked through. Remove from the skillet and set aside.

Prepare the Cauliflower Mash:

1. Cook the Cauliflower: Bring a pot of salted water to a boil. Add the cauliflower florets and garlic (if using) and cook for 8-10 minutes until soft.

2. Blend the Mash: Drain the cauliflower and transfer it to a blender or food processor.

- Pinch of black pepper
- 1 clove garlic (optional, for added flavor)

Add almond milk (or non-fat Greek yogurt), olive oil (or without), salt, and black pepper. Blend until smooth and creamy.

225 kcal, 25g protein, 8g fat, 10g carbs, 4g fiber

Tips: Add a squeeze of lemon juice to the meatballs for a refreshing flavor.

 ## 38. Citrus Seafood Salad with Kiwi & Capers

PREP: 15 MIN   COOK: 10 MIN   SERVINGS: 4

A refreshing and light salad featuring a medley of seafood, zesty citrus, and the unique sweetness of kiwi—perfect for a healthy meal.

Ingredients:

- 1 medium head of iceberg lettuce, shredded
- 1 kiwi, peeled and sliced
- 1 orange, peeled and segmented
- 8 cherry tomatoes, halved
- 200 g shrimp, peeled and deveined
- 200 g squid, cleaned and sliced into rings
- 150 g mussels, cooked and shelled (optionally)
- 1 tbsp capers, drained
- 1 lime, juiced
- 2 tbsp olive oil (optionally)
- Pinch of salt
- Pinch of black pepper
- Fresh dill or parsley for garnish (optionally)

Instructions:

Prepare the Seafood:
1. Cook the Shrimp and Squid: Bring a pot of salted water to a boil. Add the shrimp and cook for 2-3 minutes until pink and opaque. Remove and set aside. In the same water, cook the squid rings for 1-2 minutes until tender. Drain and set aside.

2. Prepare the Mussels (optionally): If using fresh mussels, steam them in a small amount of water for 4-5 minutes until they open. Discard any unopened mussels. If using pre-cooked mussels, simply rinse and pat dry.

Assemble the Salad:
3. In a large bowl, layer the shredded iceberg lettuce as a base.
4. Arrange the kiwi slices, orange segments, and halved cherry tomatoes on top.
5. Add the cooked shrimp, squid rings, and mussels evenly over the salad.
6. Sprinkle the capers across the top for a briny kick.

Make the Dressing:
7. In a small bowl, whisk together the lime juice, olive oil (optionally), salt, and black pepper. Adjust the seasoning to taste.

200 kcal, 18g protein, 9g fat, 10g carbs, 3g fiber

Tips: Drizzle the dressing over the salad just before serving. Garnish with fresh dill or parsley if desired.

 ## 39. Baked Salmon with Creamy Green Pea Purée

PREP: 10 MIN   COOK: 30 MIN   SERVINGS: 2

Salmon, packed with heart-healthy Omega-3s, pairs beautifully with this creamy green pea purée made with non-fat Greek yogurt. This balanced and vibrant dish is perfect for a nutritious dinner or a special occasion.

Ingredients:

- **For the Salmon:**
- 200 g salmon fillet
- 1 lemon (120 g), halved
- Salt and pepper, to taste
- Dill, chopped, for garnish
- Cooking spray
- **For the Green Pea Purée:**
- 200 g green peas (fresh or frozen)
- 2 tbsp non-fat Greek yogurt
- 1 garlic clove, peeled
- Salt and pepper, to taste
- Optional: 1 tsp olive oil (for a silkier texture)

Instructions:

1. Prepare the Salmon: Preheat your oven to 200°C (400°F).
Place the salmon fillet on a baking sheet lined with parchment paper. Lightly coat it with cooking spray, season with salt and pepper, and drizzle with the juice of half a lemon.
Bake in the oven for 20 minutes, or until the salmon flakes easily with a fork.

2. Cook the Green Peas: In a medium saucepan, bring water to a boil. Add the green peas and garlic clove, cooking until the peas are tender (about 5 minutes). Drain the peas and garlic, allowing all the water to run off.

3. Make the Purée: Transfer the peas and garlic to a blender or food processor. Add the Greek yogurt, and blend until smooth.
Season the purée with salt and pepper to taste. For a silkier texture, optionally add a teaspoon of olive oil.

4. Assemble the Dish: Serve the baked salmon alongside a generous portion of green pea purée.
Garnish with fresh dill and a wedge of lemon.

280 kcal, 38g protein, 8g fat, 9g carbs, 3g fiber

Tips: *Substitute salmon with trout or cod for variety.*
For a spicier kick, sprinkle chili flakes over the salmon before baking.
Add a handful of fresh mint to the purée for a refreshing twist.

 ## 40. Braised Cabbage with Chicken

PREP: 20 MIN   COOK: 30 MIN   SERVINGS: 3

Cabbage with chicken is a light yet flavorful dish that's simple to prepare. With cabbage, chicken, and a touch of tomato paste, this meal is both healthy and satisfying, making it perfect for a weeknight lunch and dinner.

Ingredients:

- 500g white cabbage, thinly sliced
- 400g chicken breast, diced
- 100g onion (1 medium),

Instructions:

1. Prepare the Ingredients: Dice the chicken, chop the onion, and grate the carrot. Thinly slice the cabbage.

2. Cook the Chicken: In a large pot or deep skillet, add a small amount

diced
- 120g carrot (1 medium), grated
- 50g tomato paste
- 1 tsp paprika
- 0.75 tsp salt (or to taste)
- 0.25 tsp black pepper (or to taste)
- 150–200 ml water

of water (1–2 tablespoons) to prevent sticking. Heat over medium-high, then add the diced chicken. Cook for about 5 minutes, stirring occasionally, until the chicken starts to brown.

3. Add the Onion: Reduce the heat slightly and add the diced onion. Sauté for 2–3 minutes until the onion begins to soften.

4. Add the Carrot: Add the grated carrot and cook for an additional 3–4 minutes until the carrot is soft.

5. Add Tomato Paste: Stir in the tomato paste and cook everything together for 2 minutes, mixing well.

6. Add Cabbage and Water: Add the sliced cabbage and pour in 150–200 ml of water. Cover the pot with a lid and let the cabbage cook on low heat for about 5–7 minutes without stirring. This allows the cabbage to soften and reduce in volume.

7. Stir and Simmer: Remove the lid, stir the cabbage with the chicken and vegetables, then cover again and cook on low heat for another 20 minutes until the cabbage is tender.

8. Season and Finish Cooking: Remove the lid, add salt, black pepper, and paprika. Stir and cook for an additional 5–7 minutes without the lid, allowing any excess liquid to evaporate. Serve Hot.

150 kcal, 24g protein, 2g fat, 10g carbs, 2g fiber

Tips: *Omit the chicken for a delicious side dish that pairs well with fish, turkey, or other proteins. Add a pinch of chili flakes for a kick of heat.*

For lunch, consider adding soups, smoothies, or even recipes from your dinner plan for variety. Aim to make your plate as diverse as possible by incorporating different textures and Zero-Point foods. Experiment with spices and seasonings to create unique and flavorful meals that keep you excited about healthy eating. Most recipes are versatile—you can swap the side dish for a fresh salad or any other option you prefer, feel free to switch between fish, poultry, or other proteins to suit your taste. A well-rounded, satisfying lunch keeps you energized and on track for the rest of the day!

4.3. SOUP RECIPES

 41. Vegetable Broth

PREP: 10 MIN   COOK: 45 MIN   SERVINGS: 6

A light and flavorful vegetable broth that's perfect as a base for soups, stews, or for cooking grains and vegetables. This versatile recipe is quick, easy, and zero points.

Ingredients:

- 1 onion, coarsely chopped
- 2 carrots, sliced.
- 2 celery stalks, chopped
- 2 garlic cloves, chopped
- Laurel leaf
- Fresh herbs (parsley, thyme)
- A pinch of salt and black pepper
- 1.5 liters of water

Instructions:

1. Prepare Ingredients: Place the chopped onion, carrots, celery, garlic, bay leaf, and fresh herbs in a large saucepan.

2. Add Water: Fill the saucepan with 1.5 liters of water.

3. Bring to a Boil: Heat the mixture over medium-high heat until it comes to a boil.

4. Simmer: Reduce the heat to low and let the broth simmer gently for 45 minutes, allowing the flavors to develop.

5. Strain the Broth: Remove the vegetables and herbs by straining the broth through a fine sieve or cheesecloth.

5 kcal, 0g protein, 0g fat, 1g carbs, 0g fiber

Tips: *For extra depth of flavor, roast the vegetables before simmering. Use immediately, refrigerate for up to 4 days, or freeze in airtight containers for up to 3 months.*

 42. Chicken Broth

PREP: 10 MIN   COOK: 45 MIN   SERVINGS: 4

A flavorful, zero-point chicken broth perfect for soups, stews, or as a cooking liquid for sautéing vegetables. This easy recipe creates a savory base without added fats.

Ingredients:

- 4 cups (1 liter) water
- 1 boneless, skinless

Instructions:

1.Prepare Ingredients: Place water, chicken breast, carrot, celery, onion, garlic, and fresh herbs into a large pot. Season with a small amount of

- chicken breast (200-250g), trimmed of fat
- 1 large carrot, roughly chopped
- 1 celery stalk, roughly chopped
- 1 onion, quartered
- 2 garlic cloves, smashed
- A handful of fresh herbs (such as parsley, thyme, and bay leaf)
- Salt and pepper, to taste

salt and black pepper.

2. Bring to a Boil: Heat the mixture over medium-high heat until it comes to a boil. Reduce the heat to low and let it simmer gently.

3. Simmer and Infuse Flavors: Let the broth cook for 30–45 minutes, allowing the flavors to develop.

4. Strain the Broth: Remove the chicken breast and strain the broth through a fine sieve or cheesecloth to discard the vegetables and herbs.

5. Optional Use for Chicken: Chop the cooked chicken to use in soups or salads, or reserve for other recipes.

10 kcal, 2g protein, 0g fat, 1g carbs, 0g fiber

Tips: *For deeper flavor, add a splash of apple cider vinegar while simmering. Use ice cube trays to freeze the broth in small portions for easy use in recipes. Use immediately, refrigerate for up to 4 days, or freeze in airtight containers for up to 3 months.*

 ## 43. Classic Pumpkin Soup

PREP: 15 MIN   COOK: 50 MIN   SERVINGS: 4

This pumpkin soup is a cozy, flavorful dish loved for its creamy texture and subtle sweetness. A perfect option for a wholesome meal, it's simple to prepare and ideal for family dinners.

Ingredients:

- 1 kg pumpkin (peeled and cut into small cubes)
- 50 g pumpkin seeds
- 1 liter vegetable broth
- 1 carrot
- 1 onion
- 1 clove garlic ·
- 1 tsp chili pepper
- 1 tbsp olive oil
- 1/2 tsp salt
- 1/3 tsp ground black pepper

Instructions:

1. Prepare the Pumpkin: Peel and seed the pumpkin. Cut it into small cubes.

2. Roast the Pumpkin: Preheat the oven to 170°C (340°F). Place the pumpkin cubes on a baking sheet, drizzle lightly with olive oil, and season with salt and spices. Roast for 40–50 minutes until tender.
3. Cook the Vegetables: In a saucepan, heat a tablespoon of olive oil. Add the chopped onion, carrot, and garlic. Sauté over medium heat until softened, about 15 minutes.

4. Combine Ingredients: Add the roasted pumpkin to the saucepan along with the hot vegetable broth. Cover and simmer for 5 minutes.

5. Blend the Soup: Use an immersion blender to puree the soup until smooth. Adjust salt and pepper to taste if needed.

130 kcal, 3g protein, 4g fat, 20g carbs, 5g fiber

Tips: *For extra creaminess, swirl in a spoonful of Greek yogurt or coconut cream before serving. Enhance flavor by roasting the garlic with the pumpkin for a deeper.*

44. # Slow Cooker Taco Soup

PREP: 10 MIN   COOK: 4-6 HR (SLOW COOKER)   SERVINGS: 6

This easy-to-make, flavorful soup combines ground turkey, beans, corn, and taco seasoning for a delicious and filling meal.

Ingredients:

- 1 lb (450 g) 99% fat-free ground turkey
- 1 can (425 g) black beans, drained and rinsed
- 1 can (425 g) pinto beans, drained and rinsed
- 2 cans (425 g each) crushed tomatoes
- 1 can (113 g) green chiles
- 2 cups (300 g) frozen corn kernels
- 1 can (300 g) tomato sauce
- 2 cups (480 ml) water
- 1 Tbsp taco seasoning powder

190 kcal, 22g protein, 2g fat, 25g carbs, 8g fiber

Instructions:

1. Brown the Turkey: Spray a large skillet with nonstick cooking spray, add the ground turkey, and cook over medium-high heat until thoroughly cooked.

2. Combine Ingredients: Transfer the cooked turkey, beans, chiles, crushed tomatoes, corn, tomato sauce, water, and taco seasoning into a slow cooker.

3. Cook: Set the slow cooker to low and cook for 4-6 hours.

4. Serve: Stir well and serve warm.

Tips: For a spicier kick, add extra green chiles or a pinch of cayenne pepper. Serve with cauliflower rice for added texture and flavor.

 45. # Creamy Cauliflower & Mushroom Soup

PREP: 10 MIN   COOK: 30 MIN   SERVINGS: 4

A smooth and savory soup with rich mushroom flavor and the creamy texture of cauliflower. A perfect comfort dish that's healthy and satisfying.

Ingredients:

- 300g cauliflower, cut into florets
- 150g mushrooms, sliced
- 1 leek, cut into half-rings
- 1 garlic clove, minced
- 100g fat-free Greek yogurt
- 500ml vegetable broth
- Cooking spray
- Pinch of nutmeg

Instructions:

1. Prepare the Vegetables: Cut the cauliflower into florets, slice the mushrooms, and chop the leek into half-rings.

2. Sauté the Aromatics: Heat a large pot over medium heat and lightly coat with cooking spray. Add the leek and garlic, sautéing for 2–3 minutes until fragrant.

3. Cook the Vegetables: Add the cauliflower and mushrooms to the pot.

- Salt and pepper to taste

Stir well and sauté for an additional 5 minutes.

4. Simmer the Soup: Pour in the vegetable broth. Bring to a boil, then reduce the heat and let simmer for 15 minutes, or until the cauliflower is tender.

5. Blend and Season: Use an immersion blender to puree the soup until smooth. Stir in the Greek yogurt, nutmeg, salt, and pepper. Mix well and heat gently (do not boil) until warmed through.

100 kcal, 7g protein, 1g fat, 8g carbs, 4g fiber

Tips: For extra flavor, garnish with a sprinkle of fresh parsley or a drizzle of olive oil. Add roasted garlic for a deeper, caramelized flavor.

 ## 46. Turkey Vegetable Soup

PREP: 10 MIN   COOK: 30 MIN   SERVINGS: 6

A flavorful and hearty soup that's light, nutritious, and perfect for any meal. This ZeroPoint recipe combines lean turkey with fresh vegetables and savory spices for a satisfying dish.

Ingredients:

- 2 stalks (100g) finely chopped celery
- ½ cup (75g) finely chopped onion
- 1½ tsp minced garlic
- 1½ (680g) ground turkey breast
- 6 cups (1.4 liters) chicken or vegetable broth
- 2 large (120g) sliced carrot
- ½ cup (75g) fresh green beans, trimmed and cut
- ½ cup frozen corn kernels
- 1½ tsp ground cumin
- 1 tsp chili powder
- 2 bay leaves
- 1 (425g) can kidney beans, rinsed & drained
- 1 (411g) can diced tomatoes with green chiles, undrained

Instructions:

1. Cook the Base: Heat a Dutch oven or large soup pot over medium-high heat. Coat with nonstick cooking spray.

2. Brown the Turkey: Add the celery, onion, garlic, and ground turkey to the pot. Cook for about 5 minutes, breaking up the turkey as it cooks, until browned.

3. Combine Ingredients: Add the broth, carrot, green beans, corn, cumin, chili powder, and bay leaves. Bring the mixture to a boil.

4. Simmer: Once boiling, cover, reduce heat, and let the soup simmer for about 20 minutes, or until the vegetables are tender. Remove and discard the bay leaves before serving.

5. Optional Garnish: Serve each bowl with a sprinkle of chopped green onions or a small amount of fresh herbs if desired.

220 kcal, 32g protein, 2g fat, 20g carbs, 6g fiber

Tips: For added spice, include a pinch of cayenne pepper or additional chili powder. Store leftovers in an airtight container in the refrigerator for up to 4 days or freeze for longer storage.

47. Borscht Zero-Point

PREP: 15 MIN   COOK: 35 MIN   SERVINGS: 4

A flavorful, diet-friendly borscht loaded with fresh vegetables, tender chicken, and vibrant beets. This zero-point recipe is both hearty and nutritious!

Ingredients:

- 500–750 g Cabbage shredded
- 300 g Chicken breast, cut into small pieces
- 1 medium (150 g) Celery root, diced
- 1 small, Onion finely chopped
- 1 medium Carrot, grated
- 1 medium Beetroot, thinly sliced
- 1 tbsp Lemon juice (from 1/3 lemon, adjust to taste)
- 1 Bay leaf
- 1 tbsp Salt, or to taste
- 1/4 tsp Black pepper
- 15 g Fresh parsley or dill, chopped (for garnish)
- 2 liters Water

Instructions:

1. Prepare the Broth: Bring 2 liters of water to a boil in a large pot. Add the chicken breast and bay leaf. Simmer over medium heat for 15–20 minutes until the chicken is cooked. Remove the bay leaf.

2. Prepare the Vegetables:
While the broth is simmering, shred the cabbage and dice the celery root. Thinly slice the beetroot and finely chop the onion. Grate the carrot.

3. Cook the Borscht: Add the cabbage, celery root, beetroot, onion, and carrot to the broth. Bring to a boil, then lower the heat and simmer for 20 minutes, or until all the vegetables are tender.

4. Season and Add Lemon Juice: Toward the end of cooking, stir in salt, black pepper, and lemon juice. Adjust seasoning to taste. Cover the pot and let the borscht sit for 5 minutes to meld the flavors.

5. Serve: Ladle the borscht into bowls and garnish with fresh parsley or dill. Serve hot.

80 kcal, 15g protein, 1g fat, 8g carbs, 4g fiber

Tips: *For added richness, top with a dollop of fat-free Greek yogurt (optional). To boost flavor, add a teaspoon of apple cider vinegar in place of lemon juice*

48. Kharcho Soup Zero Points

PREP: 15 MIN   COOK: 45 MIN   SERVINGS: 4

This modified Kharcho recipe uses chicken and chickpeas in place of beef and rice, providing a delicious and hearty Georgian-style soup while keeping it at 0 points.

Ingredients:

- 400 g Chicken breast (boneless), diced
- 100 g Chickpeas (cooked or canned, drained)

Instructions:

1. Prepare the Broth: Place the chicken breast in a large pot, cover with cold water, and bring to a boil. Skim off any foam that rises, then reduce the heat and simmer for 20 minutes until the chicken is fully cooked.

- 200 ml Tomato puree
- 1 medium Onion, finely chopped
- 1 medium Carrot, sliced
- 4 cloves Garlic, finely minced
- 1/3 Chili pepper (optional), finely chopped
- 3–4 tbsp Tkemali sauce (or 2 tbsp fresh lemon juice)
- 1 tsp Khmeli-suneli (or to taste)
- 1 small bunch Fresh herbs (cilantro, parsley, dill), chopped
- 2 Bay leaf
- To taste Salt and black pepper
- 2.5–3 liters Water
- Cooking spray For sautéing

Remove the chicken, dice it into bite-sized pieces, and return it to the pot.

2. Sauté the Vegetables: Heat a skillet over medium heat and lightly coat with cooking spray. Add the onions and sauté until translucent, about 3–4 minutes. Stir in the carrots and cook until slightly softened, about 3 minutes.

3. Add the Tomato Mixture: Stir the tomato puree into the skillet and cook for 2 minutes. Add the tkemali sauce (or lemon juice), garlic, khmeli-suneli, and chili pepper. Cook for another 2–3 minutes to blend the flavors, then remove from heat.

4. Combine Ingredients: Add the sautéed vegetable mixture to the pot with the chicken. Stir in the chickpeas, bay leaves, and simmer over low heat for 10–15 minutes.

5. Season and Garnish: Add salt, black pepper, and additional spices to taste. Stir in the fresh herbs (cilantro, parsley, and dill) and let the soup rest, covered, for 5 minutes.

6. Serve and Enjoy: Ladle the soup into bowls and serve hot.

120 kcal, 20g protein, 1g fat, 8g carbs, 3g fiber

Tips: *Adjust the sourness to your liking by adding extra lemon juice or vinegar for a sharper tang. Use freshly chopped cilantro for authentic Georgian flair.*

49. Gazpacho

PREP: 20 MIN   COOK: 1-2 HR   SERVINGS: 4

Gazpacho is a classic Spanish cold soup, bursting with the fresh flavors of ripe tomatoes, bell peppers, garlic, and onion. This refreshing dish is perfect for summer days and is incredibly easy to prepare.

Ingredients:

- 3 Bell peppers, roasted
- 1–1.5 kg Tomatoes, peeled and chopped
- 1 medium Onion, finely chopped
- 3–4 cloves Garlic , minced
- 2 tbsp Red wine vinegar (or to taste)
- Salt To taste
- Black pepper To taste
- 1–2 tbsp for garnish Olive

Instructions:

1. Roast the Bell Peppers: Preheat the oven to 200–220°C (400–430°F). Place the peppers on a baking sheet and roast for 10–15 minutes, turning occasionally, until the skins blister and soften. Remove from the oven, sprinkle lightly with salt, and cover with a clean towel or plastic wrap to cool. Once cooled, peel off the skins, remove the seeds, and slice into strips.

2. Blanch the Tomatoes: Place the tomatoes in a bowl and cover with boiling water for 2–3 minutes. Transfer to cold water to stop cooking, then peel off the skins. Chop the tomatoes into smaller pieces.

oil (optional)
- Fresh herbs (basil or parsley, optional) For garnish

3. Prepare the Vegetables: Finely chop the onion and mince the garlic.

4. Combine the Ingredients: In a large mixing bowl, combine the tomatoes, roasted pepper strips, onion, and garlic. Add the red wine vinegar, salt, and black pepper to taste.

5. Blend the Soup: Using a blender or immersion blender, purée the mixture until smooth. Taste and adjust the seasoning with additional vinegar, salt, or pepper as needed.

6. Chill the Gazpacho: Transfer the soup to a container, cover, and refrigerate for 1–2 hours to allow the flavors to meld.

7. Serve: Pour the chilled gazpacho into bowls. Drizzle with olive oil and garnish with fresh herbs if desired.

90 kcal, 3g protein, 2g fat, 15g carbs, 4g fiber

Tips: Gazpacho can be made a day ahead, as the flavors improve with time

 ## 50. Fish Soup with Salmon and Celery Root

PREP: 10 MIN   COOK: 25 MIN SERVINGS: 4

A light and aromatic fish soup featuring salmon and celery root for a healthier take on traditional fish broth.

Ingredients:

- 1 piece Salmon fish backbone (cleaned)
- 200–250 g Celery root, peeled and cubed
- 1–2 Tomato, chopped
- 1 Carrot, finely chopped
- 1 Onion, finely chopped
- 2 Bay leaves
- 0.5 tsp Salt, or to taste
- Chili pepper (optional) To taste
- Fresh herbs (parsley, celery leaves, or dill) To taste

Instructions:

1. Prepare the Ingredients: Rinse the salmon backbone under cold water, removing any fins, tail, or loose skin. Peel the celery root, carrot, and onion, then rinse all vegetables thoroughly.

2. Chop the Vegetables: Cut the celery root into large cubes and finely chop the carrot and onion.

3. Cook the Base: Place the salmon backbone in a large pot. Add the celery root, carrot, onion, bay leaves, and salt. Pour in enough hot water to cover the ingredients (about 1.5–2 liters).

4. Simmer the Soup: Bring the mixture to a boil, skimming off any foam that forms. Reduce the heat to medium and simmer for 15 minutes.

5. Add the Tomatoes: Chop the tomatoes into large pieces and add them to the pot.

6. Finish with Fresh Herbs: Chop the fresh herbs and stir them into the soup. Simmer for an additional 5–7 minutes, then remove from heat.

7. Serve: Ladle the hot soup into bowls, ensuring each portion includes pieces of fish and vegetables. Serve with optional chili pepper or garlic for added flavor.

120 kcal, 15g protein, 4g fat, 5g carbs, 2g fiber

Tips: For a richer flavor, sauté the onion and carrot in a small amount of cooking spray before adding them to the pot.

51. Seafood Medley in Fennel-Orange Broth

PREP: 15 MIN   COOK: 25 MIN   SERVINGS: 4

This elegant seafood dish combines a medley of shellfish and fish in a light, aromatic fennel-orange broth. Perfect for a dinner party or a special meal, it's flavorful, healthy, and easy to prepare.

Ingredients:

- **For the Broth:**
- 1 Fennel bulb, thinly sliced
- 1 orange Orange zest and juice
- 1 medium Onion, finely chopped
- 2 Garlic cloves, minced
- 4 cups (1 liter) Fish or vegetable stock
- 1 tbsp Olive oil (optional)
- Fennel seeds (optional)
- Salt and pepper To taste
- **For the Seafood:**
- 200 g Shrimp, peeled and deveined
- 200 g Mussels, cleaned and debearded
- 200 g White fish fillet (e.g., cod, halibut), cut into chunks
- 150 g Squid rings
- Fresh parsley or dill For garnish

Instructions:

1. Prepare the Broth: In a large pot, sauté the fennel, onion, and garlic over medium heat until softened.
Add the orange zest, juice, and fennel seeds (if using). Stir well.
Pour in the stock, season with salt and pepper, and bring to a boil. Lower the heat and simmer for 15 minutes to allow the flavors to develop.

2. Cook the Seafood: Add the mussels to the simmering broth, cover, and cook for 3 minutes until they open.
Add the shrimp, squid rings, and fish chunks. Simmer gently for 5–7 minutes, or until the shrimp are pink, the squid is tender, and the fish flakes easily with a fork.
Discard any mussels that remain closed.

3. Serve: Ladle the seafood and broth into bowls.
Garnish with freshly chopped parsley or dill. Serve hot.

200 kcal, 30g protein, 3g fat, 6g carbs, 2g fiber

Tips: Add a splash of white wine to the broth for extra depth of flavor. (optional)

52. Seafood Stir-Fry with Vegetables

PREP: 15 MIN   COOK: 15 MIN   SERVINGS: 4

A vibrant and healthy stir-fry packed with lean seafood and crisp vegetables. This flavorful dish comes together quickly and is perfect for a nutritious meal.

Ingredients:

- **For the Seafood:**
- Shrimp 200 g peeled and deveined
- Squid rings (200 g) peeled
- Scallops or white fish chunks (200 g) peeled
- 2 tsp Lemon juice (10 ml)
- 1/2 tsp Garlic powder (2 g)
- Salt a pinch
- Black pepper a pinch
- **For the Vegetables:**
- Red bell pepper 150 g, julienned
- Zucchini 150 g, sliced into half-moons
- Carrot 100 g, julienned
- Red onion 80 g, thinly sliced
- 2 cloves Garlic cloves 6 g, minced
- Fresh ginger (optional): 5 g (1 tsp), grated
- **For the Sauce:**
- 2 tbsp Low-sodium soy sauce (30 ml)
- 2 tsp Lemon juice (10 ml)
- 1 tsp Chili flakes 2 g (optional)
- 1 tsp Honey or sugar substitute 5 g (optional)

Instructions:

1. Prepare the Seafood: Toss the shrimp, squid rings, and scallops with lemon juice, garlic powder, salt, and black pepper. Set aside to marinate for 10 minutes.

2. Cook the Seafood: Heat a large nonstick skillet or wok over medium-high heat. Spray with cooking spray or lightly grease with a small amount of olive oil.
Add the seafood in batches to avoid overcrowding. Sear each batch for 2-3 minutes until cooked through and golden. Remove and set aside.

3. Stir-Fry the Vegetables: In the same skillet, add garlic, ginger, and the sliced vegetables. Stir-fry for 4-5 minutes until the vegetables are tender-crisp.

4. Combine and Season: Return the cooked seafood to the skillet. Add the soy sauce, lemon juice, and chili flakes. Stir well to coat all ingredients evenly. If using, drizzle with honey or sprinkle with the sugar substitute to balance flavors.

5. Serve: Transfer the stir-fry to a serving platter.
Garnish with fresh cilantro or parsley and sesame seeds, if desired.

200 kcal, 28g protein, 4g fat, 10g carbs, 3g fiber

Tips: *For even cooking, cut vegetables into similar-sized pieces.*
Add a touch of sesame oil for extra flavor before serving.

53. Veggie Noodles (8 types)

PREP: 10 MIN   COOK: 10 MIN   SERVINGS: 2-4

Create colorful, healthy veggie noodles with carrots, cucumber, zucchini, and more! These veggie noodles are a delicious alternative to traditional pasta. In the recipe, we will list all types of vegetable noodles. Choose one or mix several for any meal.

Ingredients:

- Butternut squash (~500 g)
- Beet (~500 g)
- Cucumber (~500 g)
- Carrot (~500 g)
- Daikon radish (~500 g)
- Summer squash (~500 g)
- Kohlrabi (~500 g)
- Zucchini (~500 g)

Instructions:

1. Butternut Squash Noodles: Select a squash with a long neck. Cut off the seedy base and reserve it for another use. Peel the neck and use a spiralizer to create noodles.

2. Beet Noodles: Choose a large beet, peel off the skin, and use a spiralizer to make noodles.

3. Cucumber Noodles: Opt for a large English cucumber. Use a spiralizer or julienne peeler to make noodles (no need to peel).

4. Carrot Noodles: Select a thick carrot, scrub it well or peel if necessary, and use a spiralizer or julienne peeler.

5. Daikon Noodles: Use a spiralizer to turn daikon radish into noodles.

6. Summer Squash Noodles: Choose a large yellow squash. Use a spiralizer or julienne peeler for noodles or a regular vegetable peeler to make ribbon-shaped noodles. No need to peel.

7. Kohlrabi Noodles: Trim off the greens and peel any rough edges. Use a spiralizer to create noodles.

8. Zucchini Noodles: Select a large zucchini. Use a spiralizer or julienne peeler for noodles or a regular vegetable peeler for ribbon-shaped noodles. Peeling is optional.

Cook or Serve Raw:

Raw: Use the noodles in cold salads or as a base for fresh dishes.

Blanched: Boil water and add a pinch of salt. Submerge the noodles for 30 seconds, then drain and rinse with cold water.

Sautéed: Heat a skillet over medium heat, lightly coat with cooking spray or a splash of water. Sauté the noodles for 1-2 minutes until slightly tender but still firm.

Season and Serve:

Toss the noodles with your favorite sauce (e.g., marinara, pesto, or tahini dressing) or add them to soups and stir-fries.

Garnish with fresh herbs, seeds, or nuts as desired.

30 kcal, 1g protein, 0g fat, 6g carbs, 2g fiber

Tips: Butternut squash & beets: Ideal for roasting before serving if you prefer a heartier flavor. Cucumber & zucchini: Best served raw for maximum freshness. Carrots & daikon: Slightly blanch or sauté for tender yet crisp results.

54. Oven-Baked Dorada (Sea Bream)

PREP: 15 MIN   COOK: 25 MIN   SERVINGS: 2

This oven-baked Dorada recipe offers a delicate, flavorful dish perfect for any occasion. The fish's light, juicy texture is complemented by fresh herbs and citrus.

Ingredients:

- 2 whole Dorada (Sea Bream) about 300-400 g each, cleaned and scaled
- 1 tbsp olive oil
- 1 lemon, thinly sliced (plus wedges for serving)
- 4 garlic cloves, sliced
- 4-5 sprigs of fresh rosemary or thyme
- Salt and freshly ground black pepper, to taste
- 1/2 cup dry white wine (optional)

Instructions:

1. Preheat the Oven: Preheat your oven to 200°C (400°F).
Line a baking sheet or dish with parchment paper or lightly grease it with olive oil.

2. Prepare the Fish: Rinse the Dorada under cold water and pat dry with paper towels. Score the skin on both sides of each fish with 2-3 shallow cuts for even cooking.

3. Season and Stuff: Rub the fish inside and out with olive oil, salt, and black pepper. Stuff the cavity of each fish with lemon slices, garlic, and rosemary or thyme sprigs.

4. Arrange in Baking Dish: Place the fish on the prepared baking sheet or dish. Arrange any extra lemon slices and rosemary sprigs around the fish for added flavor. If using, pour the white wine around the fish for extra moisture and flavor.

5. Bake: Bake the Dorada in the preheated oven for 20-25 minutes, depending on the size of the fish.
The fish is done when the flesh is opaque and flakes easily with a fork.

6. Serve: Carefully transfer the baked Dorada to a serving platter.
Garnish with fresh lemon wedges and a sprinkle of fresh herbs if desired.

175 kcal, 31g protein, 17g fat, 7g carbs, 0g fiber

Tips: *Add a sprinkle of paprika for a subtle smoky flavor.*
Swap rosemary for thyme for a slightly different herbal touch.

55. Stuffed Bell Peppers

PREP: 15 MIN   COOK: 35 MIN   SERVINGS: 4

A healthy and satisfying version of the classic stuffed bell pepper recipe, made with all zero-point ingredients. Perfect for those looking for a flavorful meal while staying on track.

Ingredients:

- 4 medium-sized Bell peppers (any color)
- 400 g Ground turkey breast or chicken breast (completely lean)
- 1 cup (~ 150 g) Cauliflower rice
- 1 medium Onion, finely chopped
- 1 medium Carrot, grated
- 2 cloves Garlic, minced
- 1 cup (240 g) Canned tomatoes, no added sugar or salt
- 2 tbsp Tomato paste, no added sugar
- 1 tsp Italian seasoning
- 1 tsp Smoked paprika
- 2 tbsp Fresh parsley, chopped (plus extra for garnish)
- Salt and pepper to taste
- 1 cup (250 ml) Vegetable stock, low-sodium or homemade

160 kcal, 28g protein, 2g fat, 8g carbs, 3g fiber

Instructions:

1. Prepare the Peppers: Cut the tops off the bell peppers and remove the seeds and membranes inside. Reserve the tops for later use as lids, if desired. Rinse and set aside.

2. Prepare the Filling: Heat a nonstick skillet over medium heat. Add the chopped onion, grated carrot, and minced garlic. Sauté for 3-4 minutes until softened, adding a splash of water if needed to prevent sticking. Add the ground turkey or chicken breast to the skillet. Cook until lightly browned and fully cooked, breaking it into small pieces as it cooks. Stir in the cauliflower rice, canned tomatoes, tomato paste, Italian seasoning, smoked paprika, and parsley. Season with salt and pepper to taste. Cook for 3-5 minutes until the mixture thickens slightly. Remove from heat.

3. Stuff the Peppers: Fill each bell pepper with the prepared filling, packing it tightly but leaving a little space at the top. Replace the tops of the peppers as lids, if desired.

4. Cook the Peppers: Arrange the stuffed peppers upright in a large, deep skillet or Dutch oven. Pour the vegetable stock around the peppers, ensuring the liquid comes about halfway up the sides of the peppers. Bring the stock to a simmer, then cover the skillet or Dutch oven with a lid. Reduce heat to low and simmer for 30-35 minutes, or until the peppers are tender.

5. Serve: Carefully remove the peppers from the skillet and place them on plates. Spoon some of the cooking liquid over the top for added flavor. Garnish with fresh parsley and serve hot.

Tips: If you prefer baking, place the stuffed peppers in a baking dish, pour in the vegetable stock, cover with foil, and bake at 375°F (190°C) for 35-40 minutes. Serve with a side salad or extra roasted vegetables for a complete meal.

56. Chicken Stroganoff

PREP: 20 MIN   COOK: 25 MIN   SERVINGS: 4

A light and creamy twist on the classic comfort food, bursting with flavor and made with wholesome ingredients. Perfect for a satisfying and nutritious meal that doesn't compromise on taste.

Ingredients:

- 600 g chicken breast

Instructions:

1. Prepare the Chicken: Rinse the chicken breast under cold water and

- (boneless, skinless)
- 2 tbsp plain non-fat Greek yogurt
- 1 tbsp tomato paste
- 2 medium onions (thinly sliced)
- 1.5 cups fat-free chicken broth
- 1/2 tsp garlic powder (optional)
- Salt and black pepper (to taste)
- Cooking spray (as needed)

pat dry. Slice into 1 cm thick pieces, then cut each piece into thin strips.

2. Make the Sauce: In a small saucepan, combine Greek yogurt, tomato paste, and chicken broth. Season with salt and pepper. Stir well and heat over low flame until the mixture begins to simmer. Set aside.

3. Cook the Onions: Spray a large nonstick skillet with cooking spray and place over medium heat. Add the sliced onions and cook for 3-4 minutes, stirring, until softened.

4. Add Chicken: Add the chicken strips to the skillet with the onions. Cook for 5-6 minutes, stirring frequently, until the chicken is cooked through.

5. Combine with Sauce: Pour the prepared sauce over the chicken and onions. Reduce heat to low and let it simmer for 15-20 minutes, stirring occasionally, until the sauce thickens slightly.

6. Serve: Serve warm, garnished with fresh herbs if desired. Pair with zero-point sides like cauliflower rice, steamed vegetables, or zucchini noodles.

150 kcal, 26g protein, 1g fat, 4g carbs, 1g fiber

Tips: To thicken the sauce further, simmer uncovered for the last 5 minutes. For a tangy twist, add a splash of lemon juice or a pinch of mustard.

57. Tofu Broccoli Bowls

PREP: 30 MIN   COOK: 45 MIN   SERVINGS: 4

A nourishing and vibrant zero-point meal, these tofu broccoli bowls are perfect for a light yet satisfying lunch or dinner. The tangy carrot ginger dressing ties all the flavors together beautifully.

Ingredients:

- **For the Bowls:**
- 2 cups cauliflower rice, prepared
- 1 recipe air-fried or roasted broccoli
- 1 recipe air-fried or baked tofu (no added oil)
- Thinly sliced daikon radish or red radish (50 g)
- Microgreens or salad greens (50 g)

Instructions:

1. Make the Dressing: Preheat the oven to 400°F (200°C) and line a baking sheet with parchment paper.
Place the chopped carrots on the sheet. Drizzle with a small amount of water to keep them moist and roast for 20–25 minutes until tender. Blend the roasted carrots with water, rice vinegar, ginger, and sea salt in a blender until smooth. Adjust the consistency by adding more water if needed. Chill until ready to serve.

2. Prepare the Bowls: In each serving bowl, add 1/2 cup of prepared cauliflower rice as the base.

- 1 tbsp sesame seeds (optional, 15 g)
- Red pepper flakes, optional
- Sea salt, to taste
- **For the Carrot Ginger Dressing:**
- 3/4 cup chopped carrots (120 g)
- 1/3–1/2 cup water (80–120 ml)
- 2 tbsp rice vinegar (30 ml)
- 2 tsp minced fresh ginger (10 g)
- 1/4 tsp sea salt

Top with roasted or air-fried broccoli and crispy tofu pieces.

3. Garnish and Dress: Add thinly sliced radish and a handful of microgreens or salad greens to each bowl.
Drizzle generously with the chilled carrot ginger dressing. Sprinkle with sesame seeds and red pepper flakes, if desired.

4. Season and Serve: Sprinkle sea salt over the bowls to taste. Serve with extra dressing on the side for added flavor.

180 kcal, 15g protein, 4g fat, 12g carbs, 5g fiber

Tips: Swap tofu for baked tempeh or roasted chickpeas for variety.
Include roasted cauliflower, Brussels sprouts, or fresh cucumber slices.

58. Braised Chicken with Spiced Pumpkin

PREP: 10 MIN   COOK: 30 MIN   SERVINGS: 2

Chicken is an excellent source of lean protein for muscle recovery, while pumpkin is rich in fiber and vitamins A and C, promoting healthy skin and immunity.

Ingredients:

- 300 g chicken breast diced
- 300 g pumpkin diced
- 1 medium onion (150 g) diced
- 2 cloves garlic (10 g) minced
- 1 tsp ground turmeric (5g)
- 1/2 tsp ground paprika(2g)
- 1 tsp olive oil (5 ml)
- 200 ml vegetable broth
- Salt to taste
- Black pepper to taste
- Fresh rosemary for garnish

Instructions:

1. Sear the chicken: Heat a deep skillet over medium heat and add olive oil. Sauté the chicken for 5–6 minutes until golden brown. Transfer to a plate.

2. Cook the vegetables: In the same skillet, add the onion and garlic. Cook for 2–3 minutes until softened. Stir in the pumpkin, turmeric, and paprika. Cook for an additional 3 minutes, stirring occasionally.

3. Simmer: Return the chicken to the skillet and pour in the vegetable broth. Cover and simmer over low heat for 20 minutes, stirring occasionally, until the pumpkin is tender.

4. Final touches: Remove the lid, season with salt and black pepper to taste, and cook uncovered for another 2 minutes to evaporate excess liquid.

5. Serve: Plate the dish on a warm plate and garnish with a sprig of fresh rosemary.

240 kcal, 30g protein, 5g fat, 15g carbs, 4g fiber

Tips: Substitute turmeric with ground ginger for a similar warm spice profile.

59. Shirataki Spaghetti & Tuna

PREP: 5 MIN   COOK: 10 MIN   SERVINGS: 2

A quick, low-carb, and zero-point dish perfect for a light lunch or dinner. The combination of shirataki noodles, tuna, and fresh lemon zest makes this meal refreshing and satisfying.

Ingredients:

- 1 pack Shirataki noodles (200 g)
- 2 garlic cloves (6 g) thinly sliced
- Zest of 1 lemon (5 g)
- 2 cans tuna in water (210 g total), drained
- 1 tbsp fresh lemon juice (15 ml)
- 2 tbsp fresh parsley (10 g), roughly chopped
- Salt, to taste
- Black pepper, to taste

Instructions:

1. Prepare the Noodles: Rinse the Shirataki noodles thoroughly under cold water.
Boil the noodles for 1-2 minutes, then drain and dry well.

2. Sauté the Garlic: Heat a nonstick skillet over medium heat and lightly coat with cooking spray. Add the sliced garlic and sauté for 30 seconds until fragrant.

3. Cook the Noodles: Add the prepared Shirataki noodles to the skillet and sauté for 1-2 minutes, mixing well.

4. Add the Flavors: Sprinkle the lemon zest over the noodles and mix. Add the drained tuna, lemon juice, parsley, salt, and black pepper. Stir until all ingredients are combined and heated through.

5. Serve: Divide the noodles into bowls and garnish with additional parsley, if desired. Serve warm.

120 kcal, 22g protein, 2g fat, 2g carbs, 1g fiber

Tips: For a spicier twist, add a pinch of red chili flakes while sautéing the garlic. Serve with a side of steamed vegetables or a light salad for a complete meal.

60. Oven-Baked Chicken Skewers with Sweet Pepper

PREP: 10 MIN   COOK: 20 MIN   MARINATION: 1 HR 30 MIN   SERVINGS: 3

These oven-baked chicken skewers are marinated in a flavorful mix of soy sauce, garlic, and black pepper, ensuring a tender and aromatic result. The addition of sweet peppers brings juiciness and a subtle sweetness to the dish, making it perfect for a light, yet satisfying meal.

Ingredients:

- 3 cloves garlic, minced
- 1 tbsp olive oil (optional)
- 100g liquid honey (optional)

Instructions:

1. Prepare the Marinade: Mince the garlic and combine it with vegetable oil and honey (optional), black pepper, and soy sauce in a mixing bowl. Stir well to create a smooth marinade.

- 1/2 - 1 tsp ground black pepper (adjust to taste)
- 80 ml soy sauce
- 3-4 chicken breasts, cut into bite-sized pieces
- 2 sweet peppers, cut into chunks
- Fresh herbs, for garnish (optional)

2. Marinate the Chicken: Cut the chicken breasts into bite-sized pieces. Place them in the marinade and toss to coat evenly.
Cover the bowl with plastic wrap and refrigerate for 30-60 minutes to allow the flavors to soak in.

3. Prepare the Vegetables: While the chicken is marinating, cut the sweet peppers into small chunks that match the size of the chicken pieces. Optionally, you can add cherry tomatoes or onion for extra flavor.

4. Assemble the Skewers: Thread the marinated chicken pieces and sweet pepper chunks onto wooden or metal skewers, alternating between the chicken and vegetables. If using wooden skewers, soak them in water for 15-20 minutes beforehand to prevent burning.
Brush the skewers with any remaining marinade for added flavor.

5. Bake the Skewers: Preheat the oven to 200°C (400°F).
Arrange the skewers on a baking tray, ensuring the ends of the skewers rest on the edges of the tray, allowing them to cook evenly.
Bake for 15-20 minutes, checking the chicken for doneness by cutting into a piece to ensure it's cooked through.

6. Serve: Garnish with freshly chopped herbs, such as parsley or cilantro, and serve hot with your favorite side dish.

250 kcal, 28g protein, 9g fat, 13g carbs, 3g fiber

Tips: Serve these skewers with a side of Pea Porridge on Water or a fresh green salad for a complete meal. If you prefer a smoky flavor, you can grill the skewers instead of baking them.

61. Baked Mackerel with Mustard

PREP: 15 MIN   COOK: 25 MIN   SERVINGS: 2

This delicious and quick recipe swaps traditional mayonnaise with zero-point Greek yogurt for a healthier alternative. The mackerel is baked to perfection with mustard and a tangy yogurt-based sauce.

Ingredients:

- 1 large mackerel (fresh or frozen)
- 1 tsp mustard (mild or Dijon)
- 1 tbsp fat-free Greek yogurt
- 1 tbsp soy sauce (low-sodium)

Instructions:

1. Prepare the Sauce: In a small bowl, mix the Greek yogurt, mustard, lemon juice, and soy sauce. Stir until smooth and set aside.

2. Prepare the Fish: If the mackerel is frozen, do not thaw before cleaning. Cut off the head and tail, remove the insides, and rinse thoroughly, removing the black membrane from the inside.

- 1 tbsp lemon juice
- Black pepper to taste
- 40 g sweet onion, sliced into half-moons

3. Slice and Season: Once the fish is fully thawed, make deep cuts across the top of the mackerel on one side. Slice the onion into thin half-moons and stuff the slices into the cuts and the cavity of the fish. Generously coat the fish with the prepared yogurt-mustard sauce.

4. Bake the Mackerel: Preheat the oven to 200°C (390°F). Place the mackerel on a lined baking tray or in a baking dish. If using a non-ceramic tray, line it with foil for easier cleanup. Bake the fish in the preheated oven for 20-25 minutes, or until it is golden and cooked through. Avoid overbaking to keep the fish moist and flavorful.

5. Serve: Transfer the baked mackerel to a serving dish. It pairs wonderfully with steamed vegetables, a green salad, or a simple cauliflower mash for a zero-point side.

180 kcal, 24g protein, 8g fat, 3g carbs, 0g fiber

Tips: For added flavor, sprinkle chopped fresh herbs like parsley or dill before serving. Leftovers can be enjoyed cold in salads or wraps for a quick lunch option.

62. Seafood Paella with Cauliflower Rice & Vegetables

PREP: 15 MIN   COOK: 30 MIN   SERVINGS: 4

This healthy take on the classic paella uses cauliflower rice for a low-carb option, paired with a medley of fresh seafood and vibrant vegetables. It's a flavorful, colorful dish that's perfect for a light yet satisfying meal!

Ingredients:

- 500 g seafood mix (shrimp, mussels, squid, octopus, and fish fillets), cleaned and cut into bite-sized pieces
- 1 medium cauliflower, grated or processed into rice-sized pieces
- 1 tbsp olive oil
- 1 onion, finely chopped
- 1 bell pepper, diced
- 1 zucchini, diced
- 2 cloves garlic, minced
- 1 can (400 g) diced tomatoes
- 1/2 cup frozen peas
- 1/2 tsp paprika
- 1/4 tsp saffron threads (or turmeric as a substitute)

Instructions:

1. Prepare the Cauliflower Rice: Grate the cauliflower or pulse it in a food processor until it reaches rice-like texture. Set aside.

2. Cook the Vegetables: Heat olive oil in a large skillet or paella pan over medium heat. Add the chopped onion, bell pepper, and zucchini. Cook for about 5 minutes, stirring occasionally, until the vegetables begin to soften. Add the garlic and cook for an additional 1-2 minutes until fragrant.

3. Prepare the Paella Base: Add the diced tomatoes, frozen peas, paprika, saffron (or turmeric), and smoked paprika (if using) to the pan. Stir well and let it simmer for 3-4 minutes to combine the flavors.
Season with salt and pepper to taste.

4. Cook the Seafood: Push the vegetable mixture to one side of the pan and add the seafood mix to the empty side. Cook the seafood for 5-7 minutes, turning occasionally, until the shrimp are pink, the mussels have

- 1/2 tsp smoked paprika (optional, for extra smokiness)
- 1/2 cup vegetable broth
- Juice of 1 lemon
- Salt and pepper, to taste
- Fresh parsley, chopped for garnish
- Lemon wedges, for serving

opened, and the squid and octopus are tender. If using frozen seafood, ensure it's fully thawed and drained before adding to the pan.

5. Add the Cauliflower Rice: Add the cauliflower rice to the pan, gently mixing it with the vegetables and seafood. Pour in the vegetable broth and lemon juice. Stir everything together to combine, then spread it evenly across the pan. Cover the pan with a lid or foil and let it cook for 8-10 minutes, or until the cauliflower rice is tender and has absorbed the flavors.

6. Finish and Serve: Once the cauliflower rice is cooked and tender, remove from heat. Garnish with fresh chopped parsley and serve with lemon wedges on the side for a fresh burst of flavor.

350 kcal, 35g protein, 18g fat, 18g carbs, 2g fiber

Tips: You can customize the seafood mix based on what's available or to suit your preferences. Crab meat, clams, or scallops are also great additions.
For a more authentic paella taste, use a pinch of saffron. If you don't have saffron, turmeric will provide a similar color and a mild flavor. For a bit of spice, you can add a pinch of chili flakes or a dash of hot sauce when cooking the vegetables.

63. Baked Chicken Patties with Cauliflower & Zucchini

PREP: 30 MIN   COOK: 35-40 MIN   SERVINGS: ~10-20 PATTIES

These juicy, nutritious baked chicken patties combine lean ground chicken with a mix of healthy vegetables like broccoli, cauliflower, and zucchini. Perfect for a light, protein-packed meal, they are easy to make and deliciously satisfying!

Ingredients:

- Ground chicken 500 g
- Broccoli 200 g
- Cauliflower 200 g
- Zucchini 200 g (grated or finely chopped)
- Carrot 100 g (grated)
- 1 medium Onion 120 g, finely chopped
- 1/2 tsp Dried garlic
- Fresh parsley 3–5 sprigs, finely chopped
- 3/4 tsp Salt (to taste)
- 1/4 tsp Ground black pepper (to taste)
- Olive oil – 1 tsp

Instructions:

1. Prepare the Ingredients: Rinse the broccoli and cauliflower, then break them into small florets. Grate or finely chop the zucchini. Peel and coarsely chop the onion, and grate the carrot.

2. Blanch the Vegetables: Bring a pot of water to a boil and blanch the broccoli and cauliflower for 2 minutes. Transfer to ice water for 2 minutes, then drain well.

3. Chop the Vegetables: Pulse the blanched broccoli, cauliflower, and onion in a blender or food processor until finely chopped. (it's better to grind in stages, separately.)

4. Combine the Chicken Mixture: In a large bowl, mix the ground chicken, chopped vegetables, grated carrot, parsley, dried garlic, olive oil, salt, and

pepper. Let the mixture rest for 10 minutes to allow the flavors to meld.

5. Shape and Bake the Patties: Preheat the oven to 180°C (350°F). Line a baking sheet with parchment paper and lightly grease with olive oil. Form the chicken mixture into small patties (about 20 pieces) and place them on the baking sheet.
Add 50 ml of water to the baking sheet to keep the patties moist during baking. Bake for 35–40 minutes, or until golden and firm to the touch.

6. Serve: Serve warm with steamed vegetables, a fresh salad, or a light dipping sauce of your choice.

60 kcal, 8g protein,
2g fat, 3g carbs, 1g fiber

Tips: These patties freeze well! Simply freeze the uncooked patties on a baking sheet, then transfer to a freezer bag for storage. Bake straight from the freezer when you're ready to eat.

 64. Cilantro Lime Shrimp

PREP: 5 MIN   COOK: 5 MIN   SERVINGS: 4

Quick and zesty, this Cilantro Lime Shrimp recipe is bursting with fresh flavors and perfect for a light, protein-packed meal.

Ingredients:

- 1 1/2 pounds jumbo shrimp (700 g), peeled and deveined
- 1/4 tsp ground cumin (1 g)
- Kosher salt, to taste
- Freshly ground black pepper, to taste
- 1 tsp extra-virgin olive oil (5 ml)
- 5 garlic cloves (15 g), crushed
- 2 tbsp lime juice (30 ml) from 1 medium lime
- 3–4 tbsp fresh cilantro (10–15 g) chopped

Instructions:

1. Clean and Season the Shrimp: Peel the shrimp by removing the shell, starting from the legs. Devein by making a shallow cut along the back and removing the dark vein. Sprinkle the shrimp evenly with cumin, salt, and pepper.

2. Cook the First Batch: Heat a large nonstick skillet over medium-high heat. Add 1/2 tsp of olive oil and half of the shrimp. Cook for 2 minutes undisturbed, then flip and cook for another 1 minute until the shrimp turns opaque. Transfer to a plate.

3. Cook the Second Batch: Add the remaining olive oil and shrimp to the skillet. Cook undisturbed for 2 minutes, then flip and add the crushed garlic. Stir gently and cook until fully opaque.

4. Combine and Finish: Return the first batch of shrimp to the skillet. Remove from heat and drizzle with lime juice.Sprinkle with fresh cilantro and toss to combine.

140 kcal, 26g protein,
2g fat, 3g carbs, 0g fiber

Tips: Use fresh lime juice for maximum flavor. For a smoky twist, try grilling.

65. Baked Sea Bass with Green Beans

PREP: 10 MIN   COOK: 30 MIN   SERVINGS: 2

This simple yet elegant dish features tender, flaky sea bass baked to perfection, paired with sautéed green beans for a light and nutritious meal. The flavors are fresh and vibrant, perfect for any occasion.

Ingredients:

- Sea bass fillets 2 pieces (about 150–200 g each)
- Green beans – 200 g
- 2 tbsp Olive oil
- 2 cloves Garlic , minced
- 1 Lemon , cut into wedges
- 2 tbsp Fresh parsley, chopped
- 1/2 tsp Salt (to taste)
- 1/4 tsp Ground black pepper (to taste)
- 1/4 tsp Paprika (optional, for extra flavor)
- Cooking spray (for greasing the baking tray)

Instructions:

1. Prepare the Fish: Preheat the oven to 180°C (350°F). Place the sea bass fillets on a greased baking tray. Drizzle with 1 tablespoon of olive oil, and season with salt, pepper, and paprika (if using).
Squeeze half the lemon over the fish and place the lemon wedges around it for added flavor during baking.

2. Bake the Sea Bass: Bake the fish for 20–25 minutes, or until the flesh is opaque and flakes easily with a fork. Halfway through, spoon some of the juices from the baking tray over the fish to keep it moist.

3. Prepare the Green Beans: While the fish is baking, heat the remaining 1 tablespoon of olive oil (optional) in a skillet over medium heat.
Add the minced garlic and sauté for 30 seconds, until fragrant.
Add the green beans and sauté for 5–7 minutes, or until tender yet still crisp. Season with salt and pepper to taste.

4. Serve: Plate the sea bass fillets and serve with the sautéed green beans. Garnish with freshly chopped parsley and a squeeze of fresh lemon juice.

350 kcal, 35g protein, 18g fat, 12g carbs, 4g fiber

Tips: For a different texture, you can roast the green beans in the oven alongside the fish. Toss them with olive oil, salt, and pepper, and bake for about 15–20 minutes, or until lightly browned and tender.

66. Stuffed Bell Peppers or Zucchini with Chimichurri

PREP: 10 MIN   COOK: 30 MIN   SERVINGS: 2

A healthy and satisfying dish with roasted bell peppers or zucchini stuffed with chickpeas and topped with a vibrant chimichurri sauce. There are two variants of the dish in the recipe, with stuffed pecans or with a zucchini boat.

Ingredients:

- **For the Vegetables:**
- 2 large bell peppers (cut in half lengthwise, seeds removed)
- or 2 medium zucchini (cut in half lengthwise, seeds scooped out to form a boat)
- 1/2 cups cooked chickpeas (drained and rinsed if using canned)
- Cooking spray or a light mist of olive oil spray
- Pinch of salt and freshly ground black pepper
- **For the Chimichurri Sauce:**
- 1 cup fresh parsley, finely chopped
- 1/4 cup fresh cilantro, finely chopped (optional)
- 2 garlic cloves, minced
- 2 tbsp red wine vinegar or lemon juice
- 1/4 tbsp red pepper flakes (optional)
- Salt and black pepper to taste
- **For the Topping:**
- Sliced cherry tomatoes or diced cucumbers for garnish (Optional)

Instructions:

1. Prepare the Vegetables: Preheat your oven to 400°F (200°C). Arrange the bell pepper halves or zucchini boats on a baking sheet lined with parchment paper. Lightly spray with cooking spray and season with a pinch of salt and black pepper.

2. Roast the Vegetables: Roast the vegetables for 15-20 minutes, until they are slightly softened but still hold their shape.

3. Prepare the Chickpeas: In a mixing bowl, mash half of the chickpeas lightly with a fork for a chunky texture. Mix in the remaining whole chickpeas. Season with a pinch of salt and pepper.

4. Make the Chimichurri Sauce: In a separate bowl, combine parsley, cilantro (if using), minced garlic, red wine vinegar or lemon juice, red pepper flakes, salt, and pepper. Stir well and adjust the seasoning as needed.

5. Stuff the Vegetables: Remove the roasted vegetables from the oven. Fill each pepper half or zucchini boat with the seasoned chickpea mixture.

6. Final Roasting: Return the stuffed vegetables to the oven and roast for an additional 10 minutes, until the chickpeas are warmed through.

7. Top with Chimichurri Sauce: Remove from the oven and generously drizzle the chimichurri sauce over the stuffed vegetables.

8. Serve: Garnish with cherry tomatoes or diced cucumbers if desired. Serve warm or at room temperature.

---

150 kcal, 8g protein, 4g fat, 22g carbs, 6g fiber

Tips: *The chimichurri sauce can be prepared in advance and stored in the fridge for up to 3 days. For added variety, you can mix in other Zero Point vegetables like diced tomatoes or spinach with the chickpeas.*

67. Detox Salad

PREP: 10 MIN   COOK: 0 MIN   SERVINGS: 4

A vibrant & nutritious dish designed to cleanse and nourish. Packed with fiber, vitamins, and antioxidants, this detox salad is perfect as a light side or a refreshing addition to any meal.

Ingredients:

- 300 g white cabbage,

Instructions:

1. Prepare the Vegetables: Finely shred the cabbage. Grate or julienne the

finely shredded
- 100 g raw beet, grated or julienned
- 100 g carrot, grated or julienned
- Juice of 1 lemon
- 1 apple, grated
- 1 clove garlic, finely minced (optional)
- Fresh herbs (parsley, dill, or cilantro), chopped (optional)
- Salt and freshly ground black pepper, to taste

beet and carrot. Grate the apple for a hint of natural sweetness.

2. Combine the Ingredients: In a large mixing bowl, combine the cabbage, beet, and carrot. Lightly massage the vegetables with your hands to soften them and release their juices.

3. Add Flavor: Drizzle with fresh lemon juice. (Optional) Add grated apple, minced garlic, and chopped herbs for extra depth.

4. Season and Serve: Season with a pinch of salt and black pepper to taste. Toss well and serve immediately, or let rest for 10-15 minutes to allow the flavors to meld.

70 kcal, 2g protein, 0g fat, 16g carbs, 5g fiber

Tips: This salad pairs beautifully with grilled protein or as a standalone snack. Store leftovers in an airtight container in the fridge for up to 24 hours.

68. Lasagna with Turkey, Zucchini, and Vegetables

PREP: 20 MIN   COOK: 35 MIN   SERVINGS: 4

This healthy lasagna swaps traditional pasta for zucchini layers, packed with seasoned turkey and vegetables for a nutritious and satisfying twist.

Ingredients:

- **For the Zucchini Layers:**
- 2 large zucchinis (400 g) sliced thinly lengthwise
- 1/2 tsp salt
- **For the Turkey Layer:**
- 300 g ground turkey or chicken
- 1 small onion (100 g) finely diced
- 1 clove garlic (5 g) minced
- 1 tsp smoked paprika (5 g)
- 1 tsp ground cumin (5 g)
- 1/2 tsp dried thyme (2 g)
- 1/2 tsp salt
- 1/4 tsp black pepper (1 g)
- 1/2 tsp chili flakes (optional)
- **For the Vegetable Layer:**
- 1 red bell pepper (150 g) diced
- 1 carrot (100 g) grated
- 2 medium tomatoes (240 g) diced

Instructions:

1. Prepare Zucchini: Lay zucchini slices on paper towels. Sprinkle with salt and let sit for 10 minutes to release excess moisture. Pat dry with paper towels.

2. Cook Turkey Layer: Heat a nonstick skillet over medium heat. Add the ground turkey, onion, and garlic. Cook for 5 minutes until browned. Stir in paprika, cumin, thyme, salt, pepper, and chili flakes. Cook for an additional 3 minutes. Remove from heat and set aside.

3. Cook Vegetable Layer: In the same skillet, heat olive oil. Sauté the bell pepper, carrot, garlic, and tomatoes for 7-8 minutes until softened. Season with oregano, salt, and pepper. Set aside.

4. Assemble the Lasagna: Preheat the oven to 180°C (350°F). In a baking dish, layer as follows:

1. Zucchini slices
2. Turkey mixture
3. Vegetable mixture
Repeat layers, ending with zucchini on top.

- 1 clove garlic (5 g) minced
- 1 tsp dried oregano (3 g)
- 1 tsp olive oil (5 ml)
- Salt to taste
- Pepper to taste
- **For the Sauce:**
- 200 ml unsweetened tomato juice
- **For Garnish:**
- Fresh parsley or basil chopped

5. Add Sauce and Bake:
Pour tomato juice evenly over the layers. Cover with foil and bake for 25 minutes.
Remove foil and bake for an additional 10 minutes for a lightly browned top.

6. Serve:
Let the lasagna rest for 5 minutes before slicing. Garnish with fresh parsley or basil.

250 kcal, 20g protein, 10g fat, 15g carbs, 5g fiber

Tips: *For an extra creamy layer, mix Greek yogurt with herbs & layer it between the zucchini. Add thinly sliced mushrooms or spinach for additional layers.*

69. Roasted Veggies and Squid Bites

PREP: 15 MIN   COOK: 25 MIN   SERVINGS: 4

A simple, flavorful dish combining zucchini, bell peppers, pumpkin cubes, and tender squid for a light yet satisfying meal. Perfect for a healthy lunch or dinner!

Ingredients:

- **For the Vegetables:**
- 1 medium zucchini, cut into bite-sized cubes
- 1 large bell pepper (red, yellow, or orange), cut into 1-inch squares
- 1 1/2 cups pumpkin, peeled and cubed (about 1-inch pieces)
- 1 tsp smoked paprika
- 1 tsp garlic powder
- Salt and freshly ground black pepper, to taste
- Cooking spray
- **For the Squid:**
- 300 g squid rings or cleaned squid tubes, sliced into rings or strips
- 1 clove garlic, minced
- 1 tsp lemon zest
- 1 tbsp fresh lemon juice
- 1 tsp fresh parsley, chopped
- Salt and freshly ground black pepper, to taste

Instructions:

1. Roast the Vegetables: Preheat your oven to 400°F (200°C).
Spread the zucchini, bell peppers, and pumpkin cubes evenly on a baking sheet lined with parchment paper.
Lightly mist the veggies with cooking spray. Sprinkle with smoked paprika, garlic powder, salt, and black pepper. Toss to coat evenly.
Roast the vegetables in the oven for 20-25 minutes, stirring halfway through, until they are tender and slightly caramelized.

2. Prepare the Squid:
While the vegetables are roasting, heat a nonstick skillet over medium-high heat. Lightly mist the skillet with cooking spray or use a nonstick pan without oil. Add the minced garlic and sauté for about 30 seconds until fragrant. Add the squid rings to the skillet. Cook for 2-3 minutes, stirring frequently, until the squid turns opaque and is just cooked through. Avoid overcooking, as squid can become rubbery.
Add the lemon zest, lemon juice, chili flakes (if using), and a pinch of salt and black pepper. Stir well and cook for another 30 seconds.
Remove the squid from heat and sprinkle with fresh parsley.

3. Combine and Serve: Once the vegetables are roasted, transfer them to a large serving dish. Top with the cooked squid rings and gently toss to combine. Serve warm, garnished with additional parsley or a drizzle of lemon juice for extra brightness.

190 kcal, 20g protein,
5g fat, 12g carbs, 3g fiber

Tips: For added flavor, sprinkle the roasted vegetables with a touch of balsamic vinegar after roasting. You can substitute pumpkin with butternut squash.

70. Baked Salmon with Herb Sauce

PREP: 10 MIN   COOK: 15 MIN   SERVINGS: 4

Indulge in this simple yet flavorful recipe for baked salmon paired with a rich, herb sauce. Perfect for both weeknight meals and special occasions!

Ingredients:

- **For the Salmon:**
- Salmon fillet (~1.5 kg)
- Salt — to taste
- 2-3 tsp olive oil or cooking spray (for brushing)
- **For the Sauce:**
- 1/3 cup (80 g) unsweetened applesauce (or 1-2 tsp erythritol, to taste) (40 g of honey)
- 1/3 cup (80 g) Dijon mustard
- 3–4 cloves (15 g) garlic, finely chopped
- 1 1/2 tbsp (20 ml) lemon juice
- 2 1/2 tbsp 40 ml (40 ml) Greek yogurt 0% fat (or 20 ml of olive oil)
- 2 tbsp (10 g) fresh dill, finely chopped
- 1 tsp dried thyme (optional)
- 1 tsp dried oregano (optional)

Instructions:

1. Preheat the oven: Set the temperature to 200°C (400°F). Line a baking sheet with foil and parchment paper.

2. Prepare the salmon: Rinse the fillet under cold water and pat it dry with paper towels. Brush each piece lightly with olive oil (or use cooking spray) and season with a pinch of salt.

3. Make the sauce: In a small bowl, combine applesauce, Dijon mustard, garlic, lemon juice, Greek yogurt, dill, thyme, and oregano. Add a pinch of salt to enhance the flavor. Mix until smooth.

4. Assemble the dish: Place the salmon fillets on the prepared baking sheet. Coat generously with the sauce, making sure it is evenly coated.

5. Bake the salmon: Transfer the baking sheet to the preheated oven. Bake for 10–15 minutes, ensuring the fish remains tender and juicy. If the center seems slightly undercooked, let the salmon rest for 2–3 minutes at room temperature to finish cooking.

6. Garnish and serve: Before serving, garnish with fresh dill or parsley for added freshness.

240 kcal, 35g protein,
10g fat, 4g carbs, 5g fiber

Tips: Keep an eye on the salmon to prevent it from drying out. It's better to slightly undercook & let it rest. Add grated lemon zest to the sauce for extra zing.

71. Zucchini Fritters with Yogurt Sauce

PREP: 10 MIN   COOK: 15 MIN   SERVINGS: 2-4

Zucchini is a low-calorie source of fiber and vitamins, while the yogurt sauce adds protein and a refreshing taste to the dish.

Ingredients:

- **For the Fritters:**
- 2 medium zucchinis (300 g) grated
- 1 clove garlic (5 g) minced
- 1 egg
- 1 tbsp chickpea flour (20g)
- **Salt to taste**
- Black pepper to taste
- 1 tsp olive oil spray (for cooking)
- **For the Yogurt Sauce:**
- 100 ml non-fat Greek yogurt
- 1 tsp lemon juice (5 ml)
- Dried dill to taste

Instructions:

1. Prepare the Zucchini: Grate the zucchinis and sprinkle them with a pinch of salt. Let them sit for 5 min to release excess water. Squeeze out the liquid using your hands or a clean kitchen towel.

2. Make the Fritter Batter: In a bowl, combine the grated zucchini, minced garlic, egg, and chickpea flour. Add salt and pepper to taste. Mix until the ingredients are evenly combined.

3. Cook the Fritters: Heat a non-stick skillet over medium heat and lightly spray with olive oil. Scoop the batter using a spoon to form small fritters on the skillet. Cook each side for 2-3 min, or until golden brown and firm.

4. Prepare the Yogurt Sauce: In a small bowl, mix the Greek yogurt with lemon juice and dried dill. Stir until smooth.

5. Serve: Plate the fritters and drizzle or serve with the yogurt sauce on the side.

160 kcal, 9g protein, 6g fat, 10g carbs, 2g fiber

Tips: *For a different flavor profile, substitute dried dill with fresh mint in the yogurt sauce. Add grated carrot to the fritter mixture for extra color and nutrients.*

72. Buffalo Chicken

PREP: 5 MIN   COOK: 4-6 HR   SERVINGS: 6

A creamy, tangy zero-point snack perfect for parties, wraps, or as a satisfying low-calorie meal. This easy dip pairs beautifully with fresh veggies or your favorite crackers.

Ingredients:

- 4 (115 g) boneless, skinless chicken breasts
- 1/2 cup (120 ml) Frank's Buffalo wing sauce
- 1/2 packet (14 g) Hidden Valley Original Ranch Salad Dressing & Seasoning Mix
- 1/2 cup (120 g) non-fat plain Greek yogurt

Instructions:

1. Combine Ingredients in Slow Cooker: Place the chicken breasts in a slow cooker. Add Buffalo wing sauce and Ranch seasoning mix. Cover and cook on low for 4–6 hours.

2. Shred Chicken and Add Yogurt: After cooking, shred the chicken using two forks directly in the slow cooker. Stir in the Greek yogurt until well combined. Cover and cook on low for an additional 30 minutes.

3. Serve and Garnish: Transfer to a serving dish, if desired. Garnish with extra Buffalo sauce or sliced green onions. Serve with celery sticks, carrot sticks, or other dippers.

92 kcal, 12g protein, 2g fat, 2g carbs, 0g fiber

Tips: *Serve with celery for a crowd-pleasing platter.*

4.5. SMOOTHIE RECIPE

73. Tropical Green Smoothie

PREP: 5 MIN   COOK: 0 MIN   SERVINGS: 1

A refreshing, energy-boosting smoothie with tropical fruits and greens.

Ingredients:

- 1 cup fresh spinach
- 1 cup unsweetened coconut water
- ½ cup pineapple chunks
- ½ banana
- ½ cup mango chunks
- Ice cubes

Instructions:

1. Place all ingredients in a blender.
2. Blend until smooth and creamy.
3. Pour into a glass and serve chilled.

90 kcal, 2g protein,
0g f, 23g carbs, 0g fiber

Tips: Add a few mint leaves for extra freshness.

74. Smoothie with Persimmon and Pumpkin

PREP: 10 MIN   COOK: 15 MIN   SERVINGS: 2-3

A delicious and healthy smoothie made with persimmon and pumpkin, perfect for a fall treat. Sweet, creamy, and nutritious!

Ingredients:

- Persimmon 2
- Pumpkin (flesh) 150 g
- Lemon juice 2 tbsp
- Orange juice 500 ml
- Vanillin to taste
- Mint for garnish

Instructions:

1. Make Pumpkin Puree: Cut pumpkin into pieces, simmer with 2–3 tbsp orange juice for 15 minutes until soft, then mash.
2. Prepare Persimmon: Peel persimmons, remove seeds, & chop the flesh.
3. Blend: Add persimmon, pumpkin puree, orange juice, lemon juice, and vanillin to a blender. Blend until smooth.
4. Chill & Serve: Refrigerate for 30 minutes. Garnish with mint and enjoy!

36 kcal, 1g protein,
0g fat, 9g carbs, 1g fiber

Tips: Add a few mint leaves for extra freshness.

75. Strawberry Mango Smoothie

PREP: 5 MIN   COOK: 0 MIN   SERVINGS: 2

A sweet and tropical smoothie blending juicy strawberries and ripe mango for a refreshing treat. Perfect as a healthy snack or breakfast option.

Ingredients:

- 1 cup strawberries
- ½ cup mango chunks
- 1 cup water or unsweetened coconut water
- Ice cubes

Instructions:

1. Place all ingredients in a blender.
2. Blend until smooth and creamy.
3. Pour into a glass and serve chilled.

70 kcal, 1g protein, 0g f, 18g carbs, 3g fiber

Tips: Use frozen mango chunks for a thicker texture.

 76. Carrot and Celery Smoothie

PREP: 10 MIN   COOK: 0 MIN   SERVINGS: 2-3

A refreshing, healthy drink full of vitamins, fiber, and the fat-burning benefits of celery. Perfect for a light snack or detox boost!

Ingredients:

- Celery stalks 2–3
- Carrot 1 medium
- Orange 1 (for juice)
- Honey 1 tbsp (adjust to taste)

Instructions:

1. Prepare Vegetables: Grate the carrot on a fine grater. Slice celery stalks thinly, including tender leaves if desired.
2. Blend: Add grated carrot and sliced celery to a blender. Blend until the mixture becomes a thick puree.
3. Add Liquid: Squeeze juice from the orange and pour it into the blender along with honey. Blend again until smooth.
4. Adjust & Serve: Taste the smoothie and add more honey if needed. Serve in glasses or hollowed-out orange halves for a fun presentation.

22 kcal, 1g protein, 0g fat, 6g carbs, 2g fiber

Tips: Swap honey for maple syrup or skip it for a lower-calorie option.

 77. Green Detox Smoothie

PREP: 5 MIN   COOK: 0 MIN   SERVINGS: 1

A refreshing & nutrient-packed green smoothie to cleanse and rejuvenate your body. Loaded with antioxidants, vitamins, and fiber, it's perfect for starting your day or as a midday boost.

Ingredients:

- 1 cup kale leaves

Instructions:

1. Combine Ingredients: Add kale, spinach, celery, cucumber, apple, lemon

- 1 celery stalk, chopped
- ½ cucumber
- 1 green apple, cored and chopped
- Juice of 1 lemon
- Ice cubes

juice, and ice cubes to a blender.
2.Blend: Blend on high until smooth and creamy.
3.Serve: Pour into glasses and enjoy immediately.

65 kcal, 2g protein,
0g fat, 14g carbs, 4g fiber

Tips: For a touch of sweetness, add a few slices of ripe banana or a teaspoon of honey. To enhance hydration, replace ice cubes with coconut water.

78. Celery, Apple, and Kiwi Smoothie

PREP: 10 MIN   COOK: 0 MIN   SERVINGS: 1

A fresh, healthy, and vibrant green smoothie perfect for weight watchers or anyone seeking a nutritious boost!

Ingredients:

- Kiwi 1 piece
- Apple 100 g (about 1 small apple)
- Celery stalk 30 g
- Salad leaves 10 g
- Fresh parsley 5 g
- Honey optional, to taste
- Mineral water (non-carbonated) 100 ml or as desired

Instructions:

1. Prepare the Ingredients: Core and dice the apple (leave the skin on if preferred). Peel the kiwi and chop it into small cubes. Thinly slice the celery stalk.
2. Blend Fruits: Place the apple and kiwi into a blender and blend until smooth.
3. Add Greens: Add the chopped celery, salad leaves, and parsley to the blender. Blend again until fully combined.
4. Adjust Consistency: Pour in the mineral water and blend briefly to reach your preferred texture. Add honey if you like it sweeter.
5. Serve: Pour into glasses and enjoy immediately for the freshest taste!

26 kcal, 1g protein,
1g fat, 6g carbs, 1g fiber

Tips: For a chilled drink, add a few ice cubes during blending or serve with ice.

79. Persimmon, Banana, and Orange Smoothie

PREP: 10 MIN   COOK: 0 MIN   SERVINGS: 2

A creamy, aromatic smoothie with a hint of cinnamon—perfect for a cozy treat or refreshing snack!

Ingredients:

- Persimmon 1 piece
- Banana 1 piece
- Orange 1 piece (for juice)

Instructions:

1. Prepare the Ingredients: Peel the banana and cut it into chunks. Remove the skin from the persimmon and any seeds, if present.

- Ground cinnamon a pinch
- Mint leaves for garnish (optional)

Cut the orange in half and squeeze out the juice.

2. Blend the Ingredients: Place the persimmon, banana, and orange juice into a blender. Add a pinch of ground cinnamon.

3. Blend Until Smooth: Blend on high speed until the mixture is smooth and creamy.

4. Serve and Enjoy: Pour the smoothie into a glass or jar. Garnish with mint leaves, if desired. Serve immediately for the freshest flavor.

63 kcal, 1g protein, 0g fat, 15g carbs, 3g fiber

Tips: To make it lighter, add more orange juice or a splash of water.

 ## 80. Berry Delight Smoothie

PREP: 5 MIN   COOK: 0 MIN   SERVINGS: 2

A refreshing and antioxidant-packed smoothie, perfect for breakfast or a light snack.

Ingredients:

- 1 cup (150 g) Strawberries
- ½ cup (75 g) Raspberries
- ½ cup (75 g) Blueberries
- ½ cup (75 g) Blackberries
- 1 cup (240 ml) Unsweetened almond milk or water
- 3–4 Ice cubes

Instructions:

1. Combine Ingredients: Place the strawberries, raspberries, blueberries, blackberries, almond milk (or water), and ice cubes into a blender.

2. Blend: Blend on high until smooth and creamy.

3. Serve: Pour into glasses and serve immediately while chilled.

70 kcal, 1g protein, 1g fat, 18g carbs, 4g fiber

Tips: Add a teaspoon of chia seeds or flaxseeds for added fiber and omega-3s.

 ## 81. Cool Cucumber Melon Smoothie

PREP: 5 MIN   COOK: 0 MIN   SERVINGS: 2

A refreshing and hydrating smoothie blending the sweet taste of honeydew melon with the crispness of cucumber and a hint of mint. Perfect for hot summer days!

Ingredients:

- 1 cup honeydew melon
- 1 cucumber
- A few fresh mint leaves
- Juice of ½ lemon
- 1 cup water
- Ice cubes

Instructions:

1. Combine Ingredients: Add the honeydew melon, cucumber, mint leaves, lemon juice, water, and ice cubes to a blender.
2. Blend: Blend on high until smooth and creamy.
3. Serve: Pour into glasses and serve immediately while cold.

60 kcal, 1g protein,
0g fat, 15g carbs, 2g fiber

Tips: For a sweeter smoothie, add a few slices of ripe pear or a drizzle of honey.

 ## 82. Refreshing Citrus Burst

PREP: 5 MIN   COOK: 0 MIN   SERVINGS: 2

A revitalizing citrus smoothie that combines the tangy flavors of orange and grapefruit with the subtle earthiness of green tea.

Ingredients:

- 1 orange, peeled and segmented
- ½ grapefruit, peeled
- 1 cup cold green tea
- 1 cup baby spinach
- Ice cubes

Instructions:

1. Combine Ingredients: Add the orange, grapefruit, cold green tea, baby spinach, and ice cubes to a blender.
2. Blend: Blend on high until the mixture is smooth and creamy.
3. Serve: Pour into glasses and enjoy immediately while cold.

70 kcal, 1g protein,
1g fat, 17g carbs, 3g fiber

Tips: Garnish with a sprig of mint or a slice of citrus for an extra fresh touch.

 ## 83. Spiced Apple Smoothie

PREP: 5 MIN   COOK: 0 MIN   SERVINGS: 2

A cozy and refreshing smoothie combining the natural sweetness of apple with the warming flavor of cinnamon.

Ingredients:

- 1 medium apple, cored and sliced
- ½ teaspoon cinnamon
- 1 cup unsweetened almond milk
- Ice cubes

Instructions:

1. Combine Ingredients: Add the sliced apple, cinnamon, almond milk, and ice cubes to a blender.
2. Blend: Blend on high until the mixture is smooth and creamy.
3. Serve: Pour into glasses and serve immediately.

60 kcal, 1g protein,
1g fat, 15g carbs, 3g fiber

Tips: Add a pinch of nutmeg or a splash of vanilla extract for extra depth of flavor.

84. Pineapple Ginger Smoothie

PREP: 5 MIN   COOK: 0 MIN   SERVINGS: 2

A tropical smoothie with a zesty kick of ginger, perfect for refreshing & energizing your day.

Ingredients:

- 1 cup pineapple chunks
- 1 tsp grated ginger
- 1 cup cold green tea or water
- Ice cubes

50 kcal, 1g protein, 1g fat, 13g carbs, 2g fiber

Instructions:

1. Combine Ingredients: Add the pineapple chunks, grated ginger, cold green tea (or water), and ice cubes to a blender.
2. Blend: Blend on high until smooth and creamy.
3. Serve: Pour into glasses and serve immediately while chilled.

Tips: *Add a splash of lime juice for extra zing.*

 ## 85. Berry Citrus Smoothie

PREP: 5 MIN   COOK: 0 MIN   SERVINGS: 2

A vibrant & tangy smoothie combining the sweetness of berries with the zesty kick of orange.

Ingredients:

- ½ cup strawberries
- ½ cup raspberries
- 1 orange, peeled
- 1 cup water or unsweetened almond milk
- Ice cubes

80 kcal, 1g protein, 1g fat, 19g carbs, 4g fiber

Instructions:

1. Combine Ingredients: Add strawberries, raspberries, orange, water or almond milk, and ice cubes to a blender.
2. Blend: Blend on high until smooth and creamy.
3. Serve: Pour into glasses and enjoy immediately.

Tips: *Use frozen berries for a thicker, frostier texture.*

 ## 86. Tropical Papaya Spinach Smoothie

PREP: 5 MIN   COOK: 0 MIN   SERVINGS: 2

A tropical, nutrient-rich smoothie that blends the sweetness of papaya and pineapple with the refreshing hydration of coconut water.

Ingredients:

- ½ cup papaya chunks
- 1 cup fresh spinach
- ½ cup pineapple chunks
- 1 cup unsweetened coconut water
- Ice cubes

70 kcal, 1g protein, 1g fat, 17g carbs, 2g fiber

Instructions:

1. Combine Ingredients: Add papaya, spinach, pineapple, coconut water, and ice cubes to a blender.
2. Blend: Blend on high until the mixture is smooth and creamy.
3. Serve: Pour into glasses and enjoy immediately.

Tips: *Add a squeeze of lime juice for a tangy twist.*

4.6. DESSERTS RECIPE

 ## 87. Mint & Melon Fruit Salad

PREP: 20 MIN   COOK: 0 MIN   SERVINGS: 4

A vibrant, refreshing salad that's perfect as a side dish, light dessert, or a breakfast topping.

Ingredients:

- Cantaloupe – 1 small (~2.5 kg)
- Honeydew melon – 1 small ~(2.5 kg)
- Seedless watermelon – 1 small (~2.5 kg)
- Blueberries – 300 g (1 pint)
- Lemon juice – 45 ml (3 tbsp, juice of 1 lemon)
- Maple syrup – 120 ml (½ cup, or substitute with honey)
- Fresh mint leaves – 20 leaves (from 3 sprigs)

Instructions:

1. Prepare the Melons: Halve each melon and remove the seeds.

2. Make Melon Balls: Using a melon baller or cookie scoop, scoop out balls from each melon. For visual appeal, use varying scoop sizes if available. Once a layer is scooped, slice off the used section to reveal fresh melon and continue until all melons are balled. Transfer the melon balls into a large mixing bowl.

3. Add Blueberries: Toss the blueberries into the bowl with the melon balls.

4. Prepare the Dressing: In a small bowl, whisk together the lemon juice and maple syrup.

5. Combine the Salad: Pour the dressing over the fruit and gently toss to ensure everything is coated. Allow the salad to sit for at least 5 minutes to let the dressing soak into the fruit.

6. Add Fresh Mint: Chop half of the mint leaves finely and mix them into the salad. Use the remaining mint leaves to garnish the top of the salad for a fresh, decorative touch.

150 kcal, 1g protein, 1g fat, 37g carbs, 2g fiber

Tips: Leftover scooped melon can be chopped and stored for snacking or smoothies. Swap blueberries with blackberries, raspberries, strawberries, or grapes for variety.

 ## 88. Mango and Yogurt "Plombir"

PREP: 10 MIN   COOK: 10 MIN + 3 HR FREEZING   SERVINGS: 4

Mango is rich in vitamin A, which supports skin and eye health, while Greek yogurt contains probiotics that aid in digestion.

Ingredients:

- 1 ripe mango
- 1 cup Greek yogurt (0% fat)
- 1 tsp vanilla extract

Instructions:

1. Peel the mango and cut it into chunks.
2. Add the mango, yogurt, and vanilla extract to a blender. Blend until smooth.
3. Pour the mixture into ice cream molds or a flat container. Freeze for 3 hours.
4. Serve by slicing the "plombir" into pieces.

80 kcal, 4g protein, 1g fat, 16g carbs, 2g fiber

Tips: Serve with mint herbal tea for a refreshing drink pairing.

89. Pumpkin Pie Cheesecake

PREP: 10 MIN   COOK: 1 HR   SERVINGS: 6-10

This delightful fall dessert combines the flavors of pumpkin pie and cheesecake for a guilt-free indulgence.

Ingredients:

- **For the Pumpkin Pie Layer:**
- 1 can pure pumpkin purée
- 3 large eggs
- 1/3 cup unsweetened almond milk
- 1/4 cup sugar substitute (like Lakanto Golden Monkfruit Sweetener)
- 1 tsp vanilla extract
- 2 tsp pumpkin pie spice
- 1/4 tsp salt
- **For the Cheesecake Layer:**
- 1 cup fat-free plain Greek yogurt
- 2 large eggs
- 1 box sugar-free, fat-free instant pudding mix (cheesecake flavor)
- 1 tsp vanilla extract
- 1/4 cup sugar substitute

Instructions:

1. Preheat the oven to 375°F (190°C). Grease a 9-inch pie dish or springform pan lightly with nonstick cooking spray.

2. Make the Pumpkin Pie Layer: In a large mixing bowl, combine the pumpkin purée, eggs, almond milk, sugar substitute, vanilla extract, pumpkin pie spice, and salt. Whisk until smooth and fully combined.

3. Make the Cheesecake Layer: In another bowl, mix the Greek yogurt, eggs, cheesecake-flavored pudding mix, vanilla extract, and sugar substitute. Stir until smooth and creamy.

4. Assemble the Pie: Pour the pumpkin pie mixture into the prepared dish, spreading it evenly. Spoon dollops of the cheesecake mixture over the pumpkin layer. Use a knife or skewer to gently swirl the cheesecake mixture into the pumpkin filling, creating a marbled effect.

5. Bake: Place the dish in the preheated oven and bake for about 50 minutes, or until the top is firm and a knife inserted into the center comes out clean.

6. Cool and Serve: Let the pie cool to room temperature before slicing. For best results, refrigerate for at least 2 hours before serving to allow the flavors to meld and the texture to set.

120 kcal, 8g protein, 2g fat, 12g carbs, 2g fiber

Tips: Serve plain or with a dollop of fat-free whipped topping for an extra treat.

90. Chia Pudding Mango Greek Yogurt

PREP: 10 MIN   COOK: 10 MIN + 4 HR   SERVINGS: 4

A refreshing and nutritious treat, packed with omega-3s from chia seeds, protein from Greek yogurt, and natural sweetness from ripe mango.

Ingredients:

- **Chia Base:**
- 2 tbsp chia seeds
- 1/2 cup water or unsweetened almond milk
- **Greek Yogurt Layer:**
- 1 cup non-fat Greek yogurt (unsweetened)
- 1 tsp vanilla extract (optional)
- **Mango Puree:**
- 1 ripe mango, peeled and diced
- 1 tbsp lime juice

Instructions:

1. Prepare the Chia Base: In a small bowl, mix the chia seeds with water or almond milk. Stir well to avoid clumps. Cover and refrigerate for at least 4 hours or overnight until it forms a gel-like consistency.

2. Make the Mango Puree: Blend the diced mango and lime juice in a blender or food processor until smooth. Set aside.

3. Layer the Pudding: In serving glasses or bowls, start with a layer of chia pudding at the bottom. Add a layer of Greek yogurt on top of the chia pudding. Spoon the mango puree on top of the yogurt layer.

4. Assemble and Serve: Repeat the layers if desired for a more colorful presentation. Garnish with fresh mango cubes, a sprinkle of chia seeds, or a mint leaf for a touch of freshness.

210 kcal, 18g protein, 5g fat, 22g carbs, 3g fiber

Tips: If you prefer a sweeter pudding, mix a few drops of liquid stevia or honey into the yogurt or chia base.

91. Baked Apples

PREP: 10 MIN   COOK: 40 MIN   SERVINGS: 4

A simple, naturally sweet dessert that's warm, cozy, and easy to make. These baked apples are tender and fragrant, perfect for a comforting treat.

Ingredients:

- 4 medium apples
- 1 tsp ground cinnamon
- 2 tbsp raisins or chopped dates (optional)
- 2 tsp vanilla extract
- 1/4 cup water or unsweetened apple juice

Instructions:

1. Preheat the Oven: Preheat your oven to 375°F (190°C).

2. Prepare the Apples: Wash the apples thoroughly. Core the apples, leaving the base intact to hold the filling.

3. Make the Filling (Optional): In a small bowl, mix the raisins (or chopped dates), cinnamon, and vanilla extract.

4. Fill the Apples: Spoon the filling into the hollowed-out cores of each apple.

5. Bake: Place the apples in a baking dish. Pour the water or apple juice into the bottom of the dish. Cover with aluminum foil and bake for 25-30 minutes, or until tender.

6. Finish Baking (Optional): Remove the foil and bake for another 5-10 minutes to caramelize the tops slightly.

7. Serve: Let the apples cool slightly before serving.

90 kcal, 1g protein,
0g fat, 20g carbs, 4g fiber

Tips: *Enjoy the baked apples as is, or add a dollop of Greek yogurt for a creamy complement. Vary the spices, like using pumpkin pie spice instead.*

 ## 92. Cocoa Delight Jelly

PREP: 10 MIN   COOK: 10 MIN + 2 HR   SERVINGS: 4-6

A light and creamy dessert with the richness of cocoa and a protein boost from Greek yogurt, made with agar-agar for a low-calorie, satisfying treat

Ingredients:

- 1 tbsp agar-agar
- 1 cup (240 ml) water
- 1 1/2 cups (360 ml) diluted Greek yogurt
- 1/3 cup (30 g) unsweetened cocoa powder

Instructions:

1. Preparing the Agar-Agar: In a small saucepan, combine the agar-agar with water. Let it sit for a few minutes to allow the agar-agar to swell.

2. Making the Jelly: Place the saucepan over medium heat and bring to a boil, stirring constantly, to fully dissolve the agar-agar. Reduce heat to low and add the unsweetened cocoa powder, stirring well until smooth. Pour in the diluted Greek yogurt, stirring thoroughly until the mixture is homogeneous. Keep on the heat, continuing to stir, for about 2-3 more minutes.

3. Forming the Dessert: Remove the saucepan from the heat. Pour the mixture into jelly molds or small containers. Allow to cool to room temperature, then refrigerate for 2 hours or until fully set.

4. Serving: Before serving, garnish with fresh berries, mint, or chocolate shavings for added flavor and decoration.

75 kcal, 7g protein,
2g fat, 6g carbs, 3g fiber

Tips: *Experiment with the spices.*

93. Cake Apple and Cocoa

PREP: 10 MIN   COOK: 35-40 MIN   SERVINGS: 4-6

A moist and flavorful cake combining the natural sweetness of apples with the richness of cocoa, kept light and healthy with Greek yogurt and no added sugar.

Ingredients:

- 4 apples
- 4 eggs
- 1 cup (70 grams) unsweetened cocoa powder
- 1 tsp baking powder
- 3 tbsp Greek yogurt (or 3 tbsp coconut oil)

Instructions:

1. Preheat your oven to 180°C (350°F).
2. Core and chop the apples into small pieces, or grate them for a finer texture.
3. In a large mixing bowl, whisk the eggs until frothy.
4. Add the cocoa powder, baking powder, and Greek yogurt to the eggs. Mix well.
5. Fold in the chopped or grated apples until evenly distributed.
6. Pour the batter into a greased baking dish.
7. Bake for 35-40 minutes, or until a toothpick inserted into the center comes out clean.
8. Allow to cool before serving.

110 kcal, 6g protein, 4g fat, 12g carbs, 3g fiber

Tips: *Perfect for pairing with coffee or tea!*

94. Chocolate Brownie

PREP: 10 MIN   COOK: 35-40 MIN   SERVINGS: 12

Packed with the natural sweetness of ripe bananas and the rich flavor of cocoa, these brownies offer a healthy treat for any occasion.

Ingredients:

- 4 ripe bananas
- 4 eggs
- 60g (1/2 cup) unsweetened cocoa powder
- 10g (2 tasp) baking powder

Instructions:

1. Preheat the Oven: Preheat your oven to 180°C (350°F). Line a baking pan with parchment paper.
2. Prepare the Batter: In a large mixing bowl, crack the eggs. Add the cocoa powder and baking powder, stirring until smooth and well combined.
3. Prepare the Bananas: Peel the bananas and lay them whole in the prepared baking pan.
4. Combine: Pour the egg and cocoa mixture over the bananas. Mash the bananas into the mixture, leaving some chunks for moisture and sweetness.
5. Bake: Bake for 40 minutes or until set and the top appears baked through.

6. Cool and Serve: Let the brownies cool for at least 10 minutes before slicing.

70 kcal, 3g protein,
2g fat, 10g carbs, 3g fiber

Tips: *Sprinkle a little flaky salt*

 ## 95. Pumpkin Muffins

PREP: 10 MIN   COOK: 20 MIN   SERVINGS: 12

These healthy pumpkin muffins are a delicious treat made with chickpea flour for extra protein and fiber, perfect for a nutritious snack.

Ingredients:

- **Wet Ingredients:**
- 1 cup canned pumpkin puree
- 2 large eggs
- 1/2 cup unsweetened applesauce
- 1/2 cup maple syrup
- 1/4 cup unsweetened almond milk
- 1 tsp vanilla extract
- 1 tsp apple cider vinegar
- **Dry Ingredients:**
- 1 cup chickpea flour
- 1 cup whole wheat flour
- 1 tsp baking powder
- 1/2 tsp baking soda
- 1 tsp pumpkin pie spice
- 1/2 tsp sea salt

Instructions:

1. Preheat the Oven: Set your oven to 350°F (175°C). Line a 12-cup muffin tin with paper liners or lightly grease it.

2. Prepare Wet Ingredients: In a large bowl, whisk together the pumpkin puree, eggs, applesauce, maple syrup, almond milk, vanilla extract, and apple cider vinegar until smooth.

3. Combine Dry Ingredients: In a separate bowl, sift together the chickpea flour, whole wheat flour, baking powder, baking soda, pumpkin pie spice, and sea salt.

4. Mix Batter: Gradually add the dry ingredients to the wet mixture, stirring gently until just combined. Avoid overmixing to ensure tender muffins.

5. Portion Batter: Divide the batter evenly among the 12 muffin cups, filling each about two-thirds full.

6. Bake: Bake for 18-20 minutes, or until a toothpick inserted comes out clean.

7. Cool: Let the muffins cool in the tin for about 10 minutes, then transfer them to a wire rack to cool completely.

130 kcal, 4g protein,
2g fat, 25g carbs, 0g fiber

Tips: *Replaces oil, making the muffins lower in fat while keeping them moist.*

 ## 96. Carrot Chocolate Cake

PREP: 10 MIN   COOK: 30 MIN   SERVINGS: ~4

A creative twist on the classic, this cake uses roasted chickpeas and carrots, offering a nutritious alternative to traditional desserts.

Ingredients:

- 3 eggs
- 10g (2 tsp) baking powder
- Sweetener to taste (optional)
- 200g carrots
- 90g (1/2 cup) roasted chickpeas
- 30g (1/4 cup) unsweetened cocoa powder

Instructions:

1. Preheat the Oven: Preheat your oven to 180°C (350°F). Line a baking pan with parchment paper.

2. Prepare the Batter: In a large bowl, crack the eggs. Add the baking powder and whisk together until well combined.

3. Add the Carrots: Peel and chop the carrots. Blend or grate them finely, then add to the egg mixture.

4. Prepare the Chickpeas: Roast the chickpeas until crispy. Cool, then blend into a fine, flour-like consistency. Add to the mixing bowl.

5. Add Cocoa and Sweeteners: Stir in the cocoa powder and sweetener to taste. Optionally, add coconut flakes.

6. Mix Well: Stir all ingredients together until smooth.

7. Bake:Pour the batter into the prepared pan. Bake for 25-30 minutes, or until a toothpick inserted into the center comes out clean.

8. Cool and Serve: Let the cake cool for at least 10 minutes before transferring to a wire rack to cool completely. Slice and serve, optionally topping with cocoa powder or Greek yogurt.

110 kcal, 4g protein, 1g fat, 12g carbs, 3g fiber

Tips: This Carrot Chocolate Cake is a delightful, healthier alternative to traditional desserts

97. Soft Pumpkin Cookies

PREP: 10 MIN   COOK: 15 MIN   SERVINGS: 12

These soft pumpkin cookies, made with healthier ingredients, are a delicious and guilt-free treat, perfect for autumn or any time you're craving something sweet.

Ingredients:

- 1 cup canned pumpkin puree
- 2 cups chickpea flour (sifted for a lighter

Instructions:

1. Preheat the Oven: Set your oven to 350°F (175°C). Line two baking sheets with parchment paper.

2. Mix Wet Ingredients: In a large bowl, whisk together the applesauce

texture)
- 1/2 cup unsweetened applesauce *(substitute for butter)*
- 1 cup Lakanto Golden Monkfruit Sweetener *(or any brown sugar substitute)*
- 1 large egg
- 1 tsp vanilla extract
- 1 tsp pumpkin pie spice
- 1 tsp baking powder
- 1/2 tsp baking soda
- 1/2 tsp sea salt

and monkfruit sweetener until smooth. Beat in the egg, then add the pumpkin puree and vanilla extract.

3. Add Dry Ingredients: Sift together the chickpea flour, pumpkin pie spice, baking powder, baking soda, and sea salt. Gradually add the dry ingredients to the wet mixture, folding gently until just combined.

4. Scoop Dough: Using a 2-tablespoon cookie scoop, drop portions of dough onto the prepared baking sheets, spacing them evenly.

5. Bake: Bake for 12-15 minutes, or until the tops are set and the edges are lightly browned.

6. Cool: Let the cookies cool on the baking sheets for 5 minutes before transferring them to a wire rack to cool completely.

100 kcal, 3g protein,
1g fat, 20g carbs, 2g fiber

Tips: Use a dash of cinnamon or nutmeg for an additional flavor boost.

 ## 98. Lemon Triangles with Chickpea Flour

PREP: 10 MIN   COOK: 25-30 MIN   SERVINGS: 9

These light and zesty lemon triangles, made with chickpea flour, provide a healthy twist on a classic dessert. Packed with protein and fiber, they are a delicious, guilt-free treat.

Ingredients:

- 3 large eggs
- Zest of 2 lemons
- Juice of 2 lemons
- 1/2 cup (120 ml) unsweetened applesauce
- 2 tbsp zero-calorie sweetener (optional)
- 1 tsp vanilla extract
- 1 cup (100 g) roasted chickpea flour
- 1/2 tsp baking powder
- Pinch of salt

Instructions:

1. Preparation: Preheat your oven to 350°F (175°C). Line an 8x8-inch (20x20 cm) baking dish with parchment paper, leaving extra paper hanging over the edges for easy removal.

2. Mix Wet Ingredients: In a large bowl, whisk together the eggs, lemon zest, lemon juice, applesauce, sweetener (if using), and vanilla extract.

3. Add Dry Ingredients: Gradually add the roasted chickpea flour, baking powder, and a pinch of salt to the wet ingredients. Stir gently until well combined.

4. Bake: Pour the batter into the prepared baking dish, spreading it evenly with a spatula. Bake for 25-30 minutes, or until the edges are golden brown and a toothpick inserted comes out clean.

5. Let the dessert cool in the dish for about 10 minutes

70 kcal, 3g protein,
2g fat, 12g carbs, 2g fiber

Tips: Add a pinch of turmeric for a slight color boost and extra health benefits.

99. Chocolate Mug Muffins

PREP: 5 MIN   COOK: 3 MIN   SERVINGS: 3

A quick and guilt-free dessert that's rich, chocolatey, and ready in minutes. Perfect for satisfying sweet cravings on a zero-point diet. (Microwave Recipe)

Ingredients:

- **Dry Ingredients:**
- 1/2 cup (70 g) chickpea flour (substituting all-purpose flour)
- 2 tbsp (15 g) unsweetened cocoa powder
- 2 tbsp (or to taste) granulated sugar substitute
- 1/4 tsp baking powder
- A pinch of salt
- **Wet Ingredients:**
- 1 large egg
- 3 tbsp (40 ml) unsweetened almond milk
- 1 tbsp unsweetened applesauce

Instructions:

1. Prepare Ingredients: Sift the chickpea flour, cocoa powder, and baking powder into a mixing bowl. Add the sugar substitute and salt. Stir to combine.

2. Mix Wet Ingredients: In a separate bowl, whisk the egg with almond milk and applesauce until smooth.

3. Combine: Slowly pour the wet mixture into the dry ingredients, stirring gently until a smooth, lump-free batter forms.

4. Distribute Batter: Divide the batter evenly into 2 – 3 microwave-safe mugs, filling each no more than halfway to allow for rising.

5. Microwave: Microwave the mugs on high for 2-3 minutes (depending on your microwave's wattage) until the cakes are firm on top and a toothpick inserted comes out clean.

6. Cool and Serve: Let the cakes cool slightly before serving. Enjoy straight from the mug or transfer to a plate for a more elegant presentation.

120 kcal, 6g protein, 4g fat, 12g carbs, 3g fiber

Tips: Adjust sweetness to taste by varying the amount of sugar substitute. Ensure your mugs are microwave-safe to avoid cracking during cooking.

100. Pumpkin Soufflé with Spices

PREP: 15 MIN   COOK: 20 MIN   SERVINGS: 2

Pumpkin is rich in vitamin A, which supports vision, and spices help speed up metabolism, making this soufflé both healthy and flavorful.

Ingredients:

- 1 cup roasted pumpkin purée

Instructions:

1. Preheat the oven to 180°C (350°F).
2. Whisk the egg whites until stiff peaks form.

- 2 egg whites
- 1/2 tsp ground cinnamon
- Pinch of nutmeg
- Pinch of vanilla extract

3. Gently mix the pumpkin purée, cinnamon, nutmeg, and vanilla extract.
4. Carefully fold the whipped egg whites into the pumpkin mixture.
5. Divide the mixture into individual baking dishes.
6. Bake for 20 minutes, or until golden brown on top

70 kcal, 5g protein,
0g fat, 10g carbs, 2g fiber

Tips: Top with a dollop of low-fat Greek yogurt for extra creaminess.

101. Mango & Kiwi Fruit Ice Cream

PREP: 10 MIN   COOK: 3 HR   SERVINGS: 2

Mango and kiwi are rich in vitamins C and A, strengthening the immune system, making this fruit ice cream a healthy and refreshing treat.

Ingredients:

- 1 ripe mango
- 2 kiwis
- 1/2 cup water

Instructions:

1. Peel and cube the mango.
2. Peel and slice the kiwis.
3. Blend the mango with 1/4 cup water until smooth.
4. Pour the mango puree into popsicle molds, filling them about 2/3 full.
5. Add a layer of kiwi slices and pour the remaining water over.
6. Freeze for 3 hours.

90 kcal, 6g protein,
1g fat, 22g carbs, 2g fiber

Tips: Swap the kiwi for other fruits like strawberries or blueberries for variety.

We've included a variety of baking and cake recipes adapted to Zero Points, so you can enjoy treats guilt-free. If you choose to use ingredients with points, try to incorporate them in minimal amounts. Enhance your desserts with berries, Greek yogurt, or a blended mix of yogurt with fruits and berries to create a delightful topping or decoration. This way, you can make your desserts not only delicious but also healthy and visually appealing. Enjoy experimenting and creating your own Zero-Point-inspired sweets!

4.7. SNACKS RECIPES

102. Baked Zucchini Chips

PREP: 10 MIN   COOK: 15 MIN   SERVINGS: 2

A light and crispy snack that's easy to prepare and perfect for guilt-free munching.

Ingredients:

- 2 medium zucchinis, thinly sliced
- 1/2 tsp garlic powder
- 1/2 tsp paprika
- Cooking spray or olive oil spray

Instructions:

1. Prepare the Zucchini: Wash and pat dry the zucchinis. Using a mandoline slicer or a sharp knife, slice the zucchinis into thin, uniform rounds (about 2-3 mm thick). Lay the slices flat on a clean kitchen towel or paper towels, and pat dry to remove excess moisture.

2. Season the Slices: In a large mixing bowl, toss the zucchini slices with garlic powder, paprika, and a light spray of cooking oil to evenly coat.

3. Prepare the Baking Sheet: Line a baking sheet with parchment paper or a silicone baking mat. Arrange the seasoned zucchini slices in a single layer, ensuring none overlap.

4. Bake: Preheat the oven to 375°F (190°C). Place the baking sheet in the oven and bake for 10 minutes. Flip each slice carefully using tongs or a spatula, and bake for an additional 5 minutes or until the edges are golden brown and crispy.

5. Cool and Serve: Remove the chips from the oven and transfer them to a wire rack to cool for 5-10 minutes. This helps them crisp up further. Serve immediately or store in an airtight container for up to 1 day.

60 kcal, 2g protein, 1g fat, 8g carbs, 3g fiber

Tips: Use a mandoline slicer for evenly thin slices, ensuring even baking. Experiment with seasonings like chili powder, or Italian herbs for variety.

103. Apple Chips

PREP: 10 MIN   COOK: 1.30-2 HR   SERVINGS: 2

A crispy, naturally sweet snack made with just apples and optional seasonings. Perfect for a healthy treat any time of day!

Ingredients:

- 2-3 large apples
- Optional seasonings:
- Ground cinnamon
- Ground nutmeg

Instructions:

1. Prepare the Apples: Wash and dry the apples thoroughly. Slice the apples into thin rounds, about 1-2 mm thick, using a sharp knife or mandoline slicer for consistent thickness. (Optional) Remove the seeds and core from the center of each slice for a more uniform look.

2. Season the Slices: Arrange the apple slices on a baking sheet lined with parchment paper, ensuring they don't overlap. Lightly sprinkle cinnamon or your preferred seasoning over the apple slices.

3. Bake the Chips: Preheat your oven to 80-100°C (175-210°F). Place the baking sheet in the oven and bake for 1.5 to 2 hours, flipping the slices halfway through baking. Remove from the oven once the edges are golden and the slices are crisp.

4. Cool and Serve: Let the chips cool completely on the baking sheet. They will crisp up further as they cool.

50 kcal, 0g protein, 0g fat, 14g carbs, 0g fiber

Tips: *Slice apples as uniformly as possible to ensure even cooking. Store in an airtight container at room temperature to maintain crispness for up to one week.*

104. Vegetable Snack with Herb Yogurt Dip

PREP: 10 MIN   COOK: 0 MIN   SERVINGS: 2

This vibrant snack is simple, healthy, and perfect for any occasion

Ingredients:

- **Vegetables:**
- 1 cucumber, cut into sticks
- 1 red bell pepper, cut into thin sticks
- 1 yellow bell pepper, cut into thin sticks
- 1 small carrot, peeled and cut into thin sticks
- 1 stalk celery, cut into sticks
- Cherry tomatoes for garnish
- **Herb Yogurt Dip:**
- 1/2 cup Greek yogurt 0%
- 1 tsp lemon juice
- 1/2 tsp garlic powder
- 1/2 tsp dried dill
- Salt and pepper to taste

Instructions:

1. Prepare the Vegetables: Wash and dry all vegetables thoroughly. Cut cucumber, bell peppers, carrot, and celery into uniform sticks for easy snacking. Leave cherry tomatoes whole for garnish.

2. Make the Herb Yogurt Dip: In a small bowl, combine Greek yogurt, lemon juice, garlic powder, and dried dill. Add salt and pepper to taste, then stir until smooth and creamy.

3. Assemble the Snack Platter: Arrange vegetable sticks neatly on a serving plate or platter. Place the herb yogurt dip in a small bowl at the center of the platter.

4. Serve and Enjoy: Garnish the platter with a few sprigs of fresh parsley or dill for an elegant touch.

70 kcal, 5g protein,
0g fat, 10g carbs, 3g fiber

Tips: *Experiment with other vegetables like zucchini or radishes for variety. Add a pinch of smoked paprika or fresh herbs to the dip for an extra flavor boost.*

105. Tropical Fruit Salad

PREP: 10 MIN   COOK: 0 MIN   SERVINGS: 2

A refreshing mix of tropical fruits with a hint of lime & mint perfect for a light dessert or snack.

Ingredients:

- 1 mango (200 g), peeled and diced
- 200 g pineapple, diced
- 200 g papaya, diced
- 2 kiwis (150 g), peeled and sliced
- 1 banana (120 g), sliced
- 50 g toasted coconut flakes
- 75 g pomegranate seeds
- 2 tbsp lime juice (30 ml, juice of 1 lime)
- 1 tbsp honey (optional)
- 15 g fresh mint leaves, chopped

Instructions:

1. Prepare the Fruit: Peel, dice, and slice all fruits as specified. Combine the mango, pineapple, papaya, kiwis, and banana in a large mixing bowl.

2. Add Citrus and Sweetness: Drizzle lime juice over the fruit mixture. Add honey if desired and gently toss to coat evenly.

3. Garnish and Chill: Sprinkle the toasted coconut flakes and pomegranate seeds on top. Add chopped mint leaves for a refreshing flavor. Cover with plastic wrap and refrigerate for 30 minutes.

4. Serve: Stir gently before serving and divide into individual bowls.

110 kcal, 1g protein,
1g fat, 26g carbs, 2g fiber

Tips: *Swap or add seasonal fruits like oranges or dragon fruit for variety.*

106. Homemade Chicken Jerky

PREP: 10 MIN   COOK: 5-6 HR   SERVINGS: 20-30 STRIPS

A flavorful, protein-rich snack that takes time to prepare but delivers impressive results. Perfect for quick, healthy bites and a great alternative to store-bought chips. These dried chicken strips (commonly referred to as «jerky») are easy to make at home by following a few key steps to ensure perfect drying.

Ingredients:

- 2 kg chicken breast fillets, sliced into strips
- 200 ml soy sauce
- Juice of 1/2 lemon or 1/3 lime
- 1 tbsp smoked paprika

Instructions:

1. Prepare the Chicken: Wash the chicken breast fillets under running water and pat dry with paper towels.
Remove bones, skin, and any visible fat to prevent burning during drying. Slice the chicken into thin strips (1.5–2 cm wide) along the grain for even cooking.

- (optional)
- 4-5 cloves garlic, minced
- 1 tbsp salt

2. Marinate the Chicken: Place the chicken strips into a resealable plastic bag (preferably one with a zip-lock). In a bowl, mix soy sauce, smoked paprika, salt, and minced garlic. Add freshly squeezed lemon or lime juice. Stir until well combined. Pour the marinade into the bag with the chicken, ensuring the strips are evenly coated. Seal the bag, removing excess air, and let it marinate for 4-5 hours at room temperature in a dark place.

3. Prepare the Oven: Preheat the oven to 55-60°C (130-140°F). If available, use the convection setting. Line the bottom of the oven with foil to catch any dripping marinade and prevent mess.

4. Arrange the Chicken: Thread the marinated chicken strips onto dry bamboo skewers, leaving 1-2 cm of space between each strip for proper airflow. Suspend the skewers on an oven rack so that the chicken strips hang freely.

5. Dry the Chicken: Place the rack with the chicken into the preheated oven. Keep the oven door slightly ajar (5-6 cm) to allow moisture to escape. Use a rolled-up piece of foil or a heat-safe object to hold the door open. Dry the chicken for 5-6 hours, checking every 15-20 minutes after the 4th hour. The jerky should be dry yet pliable, easy to chew, and not overly brittle.

6. Cool and Store: Let the chicken jerky cool completely before transferring it to an airtight container or resealable bag.
Store in the refrigerator for up to 7 days (best consumed within 2-3 days for optimal freshness)

180 kcal, 35g protein, 3g fat, 2g carbs, 3g fiber

Tips: Flavor Boost: Add cayenne pepper or chili flakes for a spicy kick.
Storage: Ensure the jerky is thoroughly cooled before storing to prevent condensation.

 107. Apple Boats with Cinnamon & Yogurt

PREP: 7 MIN   COOK: 0 MIN   SERVINGS: 2

A simple, refreshing snack combining the crisp sweetness of apples, the creaminess of yogurt

Ingredients:

- 2 large apples
- 1/2 cup (120 g) Greek yogurt (fat-free)
- 1/2 tsp (2 g) ground cinnamon
- A pinch (1 g) ground nutmeg

Instructions:

1. Prepare the Apples: Slice the apples in half and remove the cores to create a hollow space.
2. Fill the Apples: Spoon Greek yogurt into each apple half, filling the hollowed space.
3. Add Spices: Sprinkle cinnamon and nutmeg evenly over the yogurt.

80 kcal, 4g protein,
0g fat, 20g carbs, 4g fiber

Tips: *Prevent browning by sprinkling the cut apples with lemon juice.*

108. Kale Chips with Garlic and Paprika

PREP: 5 MIN   COOK: 10 MIN   SERVINGS: 2

Crispy, healthy kale chips seasoned with garlic and paprika, packed with antioxidants and vitamins to support immunity and healthy skin.

Ingredients:

- 2 cups kale leaves (stems removed, ~120 g)
- 1/2 tsp (2 g) paprika
- A pinch of garlic powder
- Cooking spray

Instructions:

1. Prepare the Kale: Preheat the oven to 180°C (350°F). Tear the kale leaves into bite-sized pieces, removing any thick stems.
2. Season the Kale: Spread the kale pieces on a baking sheet lined with parchment paper. Lightly spray the kale with cooking spray and sprinkle evenly with paprika and garlic powder.
3. Bake the Chips: Place the baking sheet in the preheated oven and bake for 10 minutes, checking after 7 minutes to avoid burning.
The chips should be crisp and slightly golden.
4. Cool and Serve: Remove from the oven and let the kale chips cool on the baking sheet before serving.

50 kcal, 2g protein,
0g fat, 9g carbs, 3g fiber

Tips: *Massage the kale with your hands after spraying to ensure even coating of the seasonings. Monitor closely while baking to prevent the chips from burning.*

109. Kiwi and Apple Fruit Rings

PREP: 5 MIN   COOK: 0 MIN   SERVINGS: 2

A quick and refreshing snack combining the sweetness of apples with the tanginess of kiwi.

Ingredients:

- 1 large apple, sliced into 0.5 cm thick rings
- 2 kiwis, peeled and sliced into 0.5 cm thick rings
- 1 pinch ground cinnamon, for dusting

Instructions:

1. Prepare the Apple: Wash the apple and cut it into rings, removing the core from each slice.
2. Prepare the Kiwi: Peel the kiwis and slice them into rings of the same thickness.
3. Assemble the Fruit Rings: Place one kiwi slice on top of each apple ring. Sprinkle lightly with ground cinnamon.
4. Serve: Arrange the assembled rings on a plate and serve immediately.

60 kcal, 1g protein,
3g fat, 15g carbs, 3g fiber

Tips: *Use red apple varieties for a visually appealing contrast with the green kiwi.*

110. Celery Sticks with Apple Dip

PREP: 10 MIN   COOK: 0 MIN   SERVINGS: 2

A crunchy and refreshing snack featuring celery sticks with apple dip. Perfect for a light bite!

Ingredients:

- Celery – 3 stalks, cut into sticks
- Apple – 1, grated
- Ground cinnamon – ½ tsp
- Lemon juice – 1 tsp

Instructions:

1. Prepare the Celery: Wash and cut the celery stalks into bite-sized sticks.
2. Make the Apple Dip: Grate the apple using a fine grater. Mix the grated apple with lemon juice and cinnamon until well combined.
3. Serve: Arrange the celery sticks on a plate and serve with the apple dip for dipping.

50 kcal, 1g protein,
0g fat, 12g carbs, 3g fiber

Tips: For a thicker dip, use a slightly baked apple instead of raw.

111. Roasted Carrots with Citrus and Coriander

PREP: 10 MIN   COOK: 40 MIN   SERVINGS: 7

This vibrant, naturally sweet roasted carrot dish is elevated with citrus zest and warm spices.

Ingredients:

- 800 g carrots, peeled and cut into sticks
- Zest of 3 mandarins and 2 lemons
- Thin slices of 3 mandarins and 2 lemons
- 1 tsp (5 g) coriander seeds, crushed
- Salt, to taste
- Black pepper, to taste
- **Optional Yogurt Sauce:**
- 1 cup (240 g) non-fat Greek yogurt
- 1 tbsp (15 ml) lemon juice
- 1/2 tsp (2 g) garlic powder
- 1 tbsp (15 g) fresh herbs (parsley or cilantro), chopped
- Salt and pepper, to taste

Instructions:

1. Prepare the Ingredients: Crush the coriander seeds with a mortar and pestle. Zest the mandarins and lemons, setting aside the zest. Thinly slice the fruits for garnish.
2. Blanch the Carrots: Bring a pot of water to boil. Add the carrot sticks, return to a boil, and cook for 4 minutes. Drain and set aside.
3. Season the Carrots: In a large bowl, toss the hot carrots with the citrus zest, crushed coriander seeds, salt, and black pepper.
4. Roast the Carrots: Preheat your oven to 200°C (400°F). Arrange the seasoned carrots on a parchment-lined baking sheet. Garnish with slices of mandarin and lemon. Roast for 35–40 minutes, flipping halfway through, until the carrots are tender and caramelized.
5. Prepare the Yogurt Sauce (Optional): Mix Greek yogurt, lemon juice, garlic powder, and chopped herbs in a small bowl. Season with salt and pepper to taste.
6. Serve: Serve the roasted carrots warm with the optional yogurt sauce on the side.

50 kcal, 1g protein,
0g fat, 12g carbs, 3g fiber

Tips: Parboiling the carrots ensures they cook evenly and caramelize better during roasting. For an extra layer of spice, sprinkle a pinch of ground cumin before roasting.

CHAPTER 5: 30 DAY MEAL PLAN

Day 1.

BREAKFASTS:
19. Vegetable Omelette with Greens
76. Carrot and Celery Smoothie

LUNCHES:
22. BBQ Slow Cooker Chicken
25. Vegetable Stir Fry
45. Creamy Cauliflower & Mushroom Soup

DINNER:
56. Chicken Stroganoff
91. Baked Apples

SNACKS:
75. Strawberry Mango Smoothie

Day 2.

BREAKFASTS:
17. Cabbage Rolls with Egg
73. Tropical Green Smoothie

LUNCHES:
28. Classic Ratatouille
32. Chicken Meatballs with Gravy & Pumpkin Puree
49. Gazpacho

DINNER:
61. Baked Mackerel with Mustard
97. Soft Pumpkin Cookies

SNACKS:
80. Berry Delight Smoothie

Day 3.

BREAKFASTS:
13. Vegetable Bake with Mushrooms
11. Berry Parfait with Greek Yogurt

LUNCHES:
24. Stewed Vegetables with Chicken in Yogurt Sauce
67. Detox Salad
48. Kharcho Soup Zero Points

DINNER:
57. Tofu Broccoli Bowls
88. Mango and Yogurt "Plombir" SNACKS
102. Baked Zucchini Chips

Day 4.

BREAKFASTS:
8. Egg White Scramble
16. Banana Pancakes

LUNCHES:
27. Fish & Chips
46. Turkey Vegetable Soup
81. Cool Cucumber Melon Smoothie

DINNER:
62 Seafood Paella with Cauliflower Rice and Vegetables
№9. Vegetable Salad with Cucumber, Tomato, and Radish

SNACKS:
106. Homemade Chicken Jerky

Day 5.

BREAKFASTS:
18. Airy Cottage Cheese Casserole with Berries
78. Celery, Apple, and Kiwi Smoothie

LUNCHES:
21. Zucchini Manicotti (Side Dish)
50. Fish Soup with Salmon and Celery Root
77. Green Detox Smoothie

DINNER:
59. Tuna Shirataki Spaghetti
93. Cake Apple and Cocoa

SNACKS:
104. Vegetable Snack with Herb Yogurt Dip

Day 6.

BREAKFASTS:
1. Cauliflower Breakfast Porridge with Berries
82 Refreshing Citrus Burst

LUNCHES:
26. Turkey in Tomato-Basil Sauce
43. Classic Pumpkin Soup
76. Carrot and Celery Smoothie

DINNER:
68. Lasagna with Turkey, Zucchini, and Vegetables
98. Lemon Triangles with Chickpea Flour

SNACKS:
109. Kiwi and Apple Fruit Rings

Day 7.

BREAKFASTS:
3. Frittata with Broccoli and Tomatoes
20. Pumpkin Spice Bread or Muffins

LUNCHES:
29. Chicken Fritters
53. Veggie Noodles
44. Slow Cooker Taco Soup

DINNER:
60 Oven-Baked Chicken Skewers with Sweet Pepper
90. Chia Pudding Mango

SNACKS:
107. Apple Boats with Cinnamon and Yogurt

Day 8.

BREAKFASTS:
14. Sweet Lentil and Green Pea Breakfast Bowl
8. Egg White Scramble

LUNCHES:
39. Baked Salmon with Creamy Green Pea Purée
85. Berry Citrus Smoothie
46. Turkey Vegetable Soup

DINNER:
62 Seafood Paella with Cauliflower Rice and Vegetables
67. Detox Salad

SNACKS:
87. Mint & Melon Fruit Salad

Day 9.

BREAKFASTS:
4. Fluffy Oven-Baked Omelet
75. Strawberry Mango Smoothie

LUNCHES:
36. Chicken Wrapped in Cabbage Leaves
77. Green Detox Smoothie
47. Borscht (Zero-Point)

DINNER:
63. Baked Chicken Patties with Broccoli and Cauliflower
81. Cool Cucumber Melon Smoothie

SNACKS:
108. Kale Chips with Garlic and Paprika

Day 10.

BREAKFASTS:
10. Sweet Black-Eyed Pea Breakfast Porridge
19. Vegetable Omelette with Greens

LUNCHES:
40. Braised Cabbage with Chicken
9. Vegetable Salad
42. Chicken Broth

DINNER:
66. Stuffed Bell Peppers or Zucchini with Chimichurri
79. Persimmon, Banana, and Orange Smoothie

SNACKS:
110. Celery Sticks with Apple Dip

Day 11.

BREAKFASTS:
5. Shakshuka
7. Lazy Cottage Cheese Dumplings with Chickpea Flour

LUNCHES:
32. Chicken Meatballs with Gravy & Pumpkin Puree
77. Green Detox Smoothie
43. Classic Pumpkin Soup

DINNER:
69. Roasted Veggies and Squid Bites
76. Carrot and Celery Smoothie

SNACKS:
111. Roasted Carrots with Citrus and Coriander

Day 12.

BREAKFASTS:
15. Smoked Salmon Omelette with Creamy Cheese
12. Pancakes

LUNCHES:
34. Braised Cabbage with Asparagus, Tomato Paste & Ground Turkey
78. Celery, Apple, Kiwi Smoothie
45. Creamy Cauliflower and Mushroom Soup

DINNER:
72. Buffalo Chicken
53. Veggie Noodles

SNACKS:
104. Vegetable Snack with Herb

Day 13.

BREAKFASTS:
6. Vegetable Casserole with Zucchini and Spinach
11. Berry Parfait with Greek Yogurt

LUNCHES:
35. Cod Stewed in Tomato Sauce
49. Gazpacho
75. Strawberry Mango Smoothie

DINNER:
55. Stuffed Bell Peppers
6. Vegetable Casserole with Zucchini and Spinach

SNACKS:
89. Pumpkin Pie Cheesecake

Day 14.

BREAKFASTS:
1. Cauliflower Breakfast Porridge with Berries
4. Fluffy Oven-Baked Omelet

LUNCHES:
39. Baked Salmon with Creamy Green Pea Purée
41. Vegetable Broth
82 Refreshing Citrus Burst

DINNER:
64. Cilantro Lime Shrimp
9. Vegetable Salad with Cucumber, Tomato, and Radish

SNACKS:
92. Cocoa Delight Jelly

Day 15.

BREAKFASTS:
2. Turkey, Spinach & Broccoli Omelette
16. Banana Pancakes

LUNCHES:
26. Turkey in Tomato-Basil Sauce
47. Borscht Zero-Point
84. Pineapple Ginger Smoothie

DINNER:
57. Tofu Broccoli Bowls
87. Mint & Melon Fruit Salad

SNACKS:
102. Baked Zucchini Chips

Day 16.

BREAKFASTS:
18. Airy Cottage Cheese Casserole with Berries
5. Shakshuka

LUNCHES:
25. Vegetable Stir Fry
81. Cool Cucumber Melon Smoothie
91. Baked Apples

DINNER:
57. Tofu Broccoli Bowls
67. Detox Salad

SNACKS
110. Celery Sticks with Apple Dip

Day 17.

BREAKFASTS:
13. Vegetable Bake with Mushrooms
20. Pumpkin Spice Bread or Muffins

LUNCHES:
37. Fish Meatballs with Cauliflower Mash
77. Green Detox Smoothie
51. Seafood Medley Broth

DINNER:
52. Seafood Stir-Fry with Vegetables
№9. Vegetable Salad

SNACKS
105. Tropical Fruit Salad

Day 18.

BREAKFASTS:
10. Sweet Black-Eyed Pea Breakfast Porridge
82 Refreshing Citrus Burst

LUNCHES:
24. Stewed Vegetables with Chicken in Yogurt Sauce
76. Carrot and Celery Smoothie
88. Mango and Yogurt "Plombir"

DINNER:
71. Zucchini Fritters with Yogurt Sauce
29. Chicken Fritters

SNACKS:
109. Kiwi and Apple Fruit Rings

Day 19.

BREAKFASTS:
2. Turkey, Spinach & Broccoli Omelette
90. Chia Pudding Mango Greek Yogurt

LUNCHES:
33. Tofu Stir-Fry with Vegetables
83 Spiced Apple Smoothie
44. Slow Cooker Taco Soup

DINNER:
62 Seafood Paella with Cauliflower Rice and Vegetables
67. Detox Salad

SNACKS:
94. Chocolate Brownie

Day 20.

BREAKFASTS:
17. Cabbage Rolls with Egg
11. Berry Parfait with Greek Yogurt

LUNCHES:
32. Chicken Meatballs with Gravy & Pumpkin Puree
45. Creamy Cauliflower and Mushroom Sou
81. Cool Cucumber Melon Smoothie

DINNER:
Baked Chicken Patties with Broccoli and Cauliflower
79. Persimmon, Banana, and Orange Smoothie

SNACKS:
106. Homemade Chicken Jerky

Day 21.

BREAKFASTS:
5. Shakshuka Recipe
9. Vegetable Salad with Cucumber, Tomato, and Radish

LUNCHES:
23. Cilantro Lime Cauliflower Rice
70. Baked Salmon & Herb Sauce
50. Fish Soup with Salmon and Celery Root

DINNER:
63. Baked Chicken Patties with Broccoli and Cauliflower
57. Tofu Broccoli Bowls

SNACKS:
101. Mango & Kiwi Fruit Ice Cream

Day 22.

BREAKFASTS:
10. Sweet Black-Eyed Pea Breakfast Porridge
8. Egg White Scramble

LUNCHES:
40. Braised Cabbage with Chicken
75. Strawberry Mango Smoothie
48. Kharcho Soup Zero Points

DINNER:
60. Oven-Baked Chicken Skewers with Sweet Pepper
100. Pumpkin Soufflé with Spices

SNACKS:
91. Baked Apples

Day 23.

BREAKFASTS:
16. Banana Pancakes
2. Turkey, Broccoli & Omelette

LUNCHES:
31. Vegetable Salad with Chicken Breast & Lemon Dressing
21. Zucchini Manicotti (Side Dish)
45. Creamy Cauliflower and Mushroom Soup

DINNER:
65 Baked Sea Bass & Green Beans
9. Vegetable Salad with Cucumber, Tomato, and Radish

SNACKS:
86. Tropical Papaya Spinach Smoothie

Day 24.

BREAKFASTS:
18. Airy Cottage Cheese Casserole with Berries
5. Shakshuka

LUNCHES:
27. Fish & Chips
74. Smoothie with Persimmon and Pumpkin Puree
43. Classic Pumpkin Soup

DINNER:
52. Seafood Stir-Fry with Vegetables
91. Baked Apples

SNACKS:
107. Apple Boats with Cinnamon and Yogurt

Day 25.

BREAKFASTS:
4. Fluffy Oven-Baked Omelet
16. Banana Pancakes

LUNCHES:
24. Stewed Vegetables with Chicken in Yogurt Sauce
82 Refreshing Citrus Burst
42. Chicken Broth

DINNER:
53. Veggie Noodles
61. Baked Mackerel with Mustard

SNACKS
93. Cake Apple and Cocoa

Day 26.

BREAKFASTS:
15. Smoked Salmon Omelette with Creamy Cheese
84. Pineapple Ginger Smoothie

LUNCHES:
23. Cilantro Lime Cauliflower Rice
80. Berry Delight Smoothie
51. Seafood Medley in Fennel-Orange Broth

DINNER:
69. Roasted Veggies & Squid Bites
77. Green Detox Smoothie

SNACKS:
103. Apple Chips

Day 27.

BREAKFASTS:
19. Vegetable Omelette with Greens
75. Strawberry Mango Smoothie

LUNCHES:
26. Turkey in Tomato-Basil Sauce
67. Detox Salad
46. Turkey Vegetable Soup

DINNER:
56. Chicken Stroganoff
74. Smoothie with Persimmon and Pumpkin Puree

SNACKS:
104. Vegetable Snack with Herb Yogurt Dip

Day 28.

BREAKFASTS:
7. Lazy Cottage Cheese Dumplings with Chickpea Flour
2. Turkey, Spinach & Broccoli Omelette

LUNCHES:
30. Spaghetti Squash
29. Chicken Fritters
9. Vegetable Salad with Cucumber, Tomato, and Radish

DINNER:
65 Baked Sea Bass with Green Beans
86. Tropical Papaya Spinach Smoothie

SNACKS:
92. Cocoa Delight Jelly

Day 29.

BREAKFASTS:
10. Sweet Black-Eyed Pea Breakfast Porridge
8. Egg White Scramble

LUNCHES:
38 Citrus Seafood Salad with Kiwi and Capers
81. Cool Cucumber Melon Smoothie
44. Slow Cooker Taco Soup

DINNER:
59. Tuna Shirataki Spaghetti
98. Lemon Triangles with Chickpea Flour

SNACKS:
111. Roasted Carrots with Citrus and Coriander

Day 30.

BREAKFASTS:
1. Cauliflower Breakfast Porridge with Berries
16. Banana Pancakes

LUNCHES:
32. Chicken Meatballs with Gravy & Pumpkin Puree
31. Vegetable Salad with Chicken Breast & Lemon Dressing
46. Turkey Vegetable Soup

DINNER:
54. Oven-Baked Dorada (Sea Bream)
73. Tropical Green Smoothie

SNACKS:
88. Mango and Yogurt "Plombir"

We've provided you with a meal plan template, but feel free to customize it by adding more salads, fruits, and vegetables as snacks or as complements to your main meals. Choose recipes you enjoy and create a meal plan that works best for you.

CHAPTER 6: BONUS MATERIALS

Thank You for Reading!

We hope you enjoyed this book and found it helpful on your journey. As a token of our appreciation, we've prepared exclusive bonus materials just for you.

To access your free bonus materials:
1. Scan the QR code below using your phone's camera.
2. Fill in the short form with your details.
3. Instantly download your bonus resources!

Thank you for your support, and we wish you great success on your journey!

PLEASE, LEAVE A REVIEW FOR AMAZON

Your Amazon reviews play an important role for our business. Please support us by leaving a review on Amazon!

Just search for this book on Amazon, scroll down to the customer reviews section and share your thoughts. We really appreciate your opinion.

Thank you so much for your support!
